"To prepare today's students for tomorrow's world, we must create authentic, personalized, real-world learning opportunities for all students. To unleash students' full potential and to ultimately create Bold Schools, school leaders must harness the power of technology to amplify great teaching practices. This book provides a dynamic blueprint to implementing high-quality blended learning experiences for all kids and is an excellent tool for every school leader's toolkit."

—Thomas C. Murray
Director of Innovation, Future Ready Schools; 2017 Education Thought Leader of the Year; and Co-Author, *Learning Transformed: 8 Keys to Designing Tomorrow's Schools, Today* and *Leading Professional Learning: Tools to Connect and Empower Teachers*

"*Bold School* is the text every educator needs. Visit any school, and you will see the struggle: educators trying to balance what we know works with what we think can take learning to the next level in the 21st century. Based on years of masterful teaching and instructional coaching, Weston bridges this gap for us, creating an engaging, practical, and empowering guide for teachers and coaches. Weston has given us two gifts with *Bold School*: the gift of research-based permission to do what we know is best and the gift of guidance to take bold, blended risks. Game on!"

—Chase Mielke
Michigan Teacher of the Year Nominee; Creator of Award Winning Positive Psychology Programming for At-Risk Students; Blogger Extraordinaire

"Weston steps us through the looking glass of effective blended learning with his unique experiences, relevant anecdotes, and application of research. He challenges innovation and change head on. *Bold School* is a must-read for all educators who want to transform the classroom."

—Nathan Lang
Co-Founder of #LeadUpChat and #DivergEd and former Education Strategist at NASA

"*Bold School* strikes a delicate balance of honoring the past while also looking to the future of education. The conversational style was fun to read and yet is packed with good pedagogy and sage advice. It's valuable reading for the novice or experienced educator!"

—David Guerin
National Blue Ribbon School Principal and National Digital Principal; National Association of Secondary School Principals

"Many education leaders are talking about the power and opportunities new and emerging technologies bring to education. In *Bold School*, Weston shares practical strategies to actually realize that power and those opportunities. A great solution-filled book for all educators."

—Dr. Bill Daggett
Founder and Chairman, International Center for Leadership in Education and Creator of the Rigor/Relevance Framework®

"Weston's ability to translate the promise of blended practices into reality within classrooms is the best I have even seen. As an educator, Weston is gifted at supporting teachers in their transformation of teaching and learning environments, helping to design authentic, interactive, and technology-rich experiences that ensure students are future ready. As an author, Weston proves in this book that he is also gifted at describing instructional strategies that districts, schools, and teachers can use to transition from old to bold."

—Dr. Chris Weber
Leading RTI Influencer and Best-Selling Author of *Pyramid Response to Intervention; RTI is a Verb;* and *RTI Roadmap*

"After reading *Bold School*, I was invigorated and excited! Weston does an excellent job of sharing his heart, as well as great ideas and resources. When I read books like this, I'm thankful we have passionate educators out there willing to share their voices to help shape and change our field! This book is excellent!"

—Todd Nesloney
White House Champion of Change, National School Board Association 20 to Watch, and Co-Author of *Kids Deserve It: Pushing Boundaries and Challenging Conventional Thinking*

"Weston Kieschnick hits it out of the park in *Bold School*. He does a masterful job of validating the work of teachers by reminding us that in our haste to innovate we have forgotten about the things great teachers do. Kieschnick provides us with specific examples and practical stories that demonstrate great teaching can still rely on "old school" techniques while layering new technologies into instruction. This book is filled with new truths that will inspire you to blend and shift your teaching back onto the right path."

—Jimmy Casas
National Secondary Principal of the Year, Co-Author,
What Connected Educators Do Differently and *Start. Right. Now.*

"Bold School...needs to be an essential part of every educator's tool box."
—JOHN HATTIE

BOLD SCHOOL

OLD SCHOOL WISDOM + NEW SCHOOL TECHNOLOGIES = BLENDED LEARNING THAT WORKS

WESTON KIESCHNICK

FOREWORD BY JAIME CASAP, EDUCATION EVANGELIST, GOOGLE

Published by International Center for Leadership in Education, Inc., a division of Houghton Mifflin Harcourt.

Printed in the U.S.A.

ISBN-13: 978-1-328-01626-3
ISBN-10: 1-328-01626-9

8 9 7239 26 25 24 23 22
4500839659   ABC

International Center for Leadership in Education
1587 Route 146
Rexford, New York 12148
(518) 399-2776
fax (518) 399-7607
www.LeaderEd.com
info@LeaderEd.com

DEDICATION

To my wife, Molly. Whenever I feel proud about writing one whole book, I remind myself that you made two whole people—and in less time. You make me better every day. I love you.

To my children, Charlotte and Everett. This book and my life are dedicated to you. I teach teachers in the hope that you and your peers will learn in schools that are filled with joyful, engaging, and successful learning. I love you more than you can possibly imagine.

To my parents who taught me that grit, determination, and the pursuit of knowledge are the keys that unlock life's closed doors. I love you both.

ACKNOWLEDGMENTS

One person doesn't write a book. Every literary accomplishment is the byproduct of a team of people who brought the author to a place of publication. The same is true for me. I owe a debt of gratitude to the many people who made this book possible. To the masterful educators who helped me cultivate a love of teaching and the competency to do it well: Kathryn Knox, Kirk Daddow, Lisa DeSilva, Nicole Grant, Kalmar Richards, Chase Mielke, and Amy Smith. You are models of academic excellence to which I aspire.

Special gratitude is due to Kelly Griego, without whom this book would not be possible. I stand in awe of your brilliance.

To Wendi Pillars and Michael Gordon: thank you for making *Bold School* come to life with your creative contributions.

To my friends and colleagues at the International Center for Leadership in Education: Sue Gendron, Bill Daggett, Eric Sheninger, and Chris Weber. I am honored and humbled to work alongside you. Children who may never know your names benefit in ways they will likely never understand because of your relentless desire and passion to make school a place that *works* for them. I'd be remiss if I didn't also acknowledge the entire staff at Houghton Mifflin Harcourt. Everyone in the organization is singularly committed to providing robust academic solutions for our schools so that students can achieve at the highest possible levels.

Finally, for all of the educators around the world who work tirelessly to share wisdom, embrace innovation, and ensure every child can name at least one adult who cares about them. You are owed so much more than this book. Thank you for devoting your increasingly scarce time to reading it. The gratitude I feel is overwhelming.

Additional thanks to the reviewers of *Bold School* and friends and colleagues whose support and feedback made this book infinitely better than I could have on my own: Kris Ross, Linda Lucey, Aimee Corrigan, and Brent Hartsell.

To Jaime Casap: thank you for the powerful foreword you contributed to this book. The value it adds for readers is immeasurable. Your work serves as a reminder to all of us that we need to stop pointing fingers and start asking questions.

CONTENTS

FOREWORD

I am not on the "education is broken" bandwagon. Education disrupts poverty. Education provides hope and unlocks kids' potential. Education is the reason why I am where I am today. If you understand the history of education, you see we have done some amazing things. In 1910, the high school graduation rate in this country was 8 percent.[1] The content we teach students today is so much richer and far more complex than it was 100 years ago—and yet we just logged our highest graduation rate on record. In 2014–15, 83 percent[2] of our high school students graduated. Talk about progress. Talk about success.

From where I sit, three things need to change so that we can have a more productive conversation about how best to educate today's students:

1. We must give credit where credit is due;
2. We must stop pointing fingers and instead ask questions so logical dialogue can be had; and
3. Technology needs to become a more invisible, organic, seamless part of teaching and learning.

As Google's Education Evangelist, I have had the privilege of working with educators for 10 years. Before this, I spent six years at Accenture, which afforded me the opportunity to work in all types of industries. I worked in the banking industry, the

---

[1] Goldin, 1998. America's graduation from high school: The evolution and spread of secondary schooling in the twentieth century. *Journal of Economic History* 58(2): 345–374.
[2] U.S. Department of Education. (2015, December 15). *U.S. High School Graduation Rate Hits New Record High.* Retrieved from https://www.ed.gov/news/press-releases/us-high-school-graduation-rate-hits-new-record-high

government industry, the energy industry, and the electronics and high tech industry. Unequivocally, teachers are the most passionate and dedicated workforce I have ever had the pleasure to work with. Their commitment to their customer—students—is unparalleled.

Unequivocally, teachers, you are and have always been amazing. We built this superpower country on the back of our education system. It's always interesting to me—even somewhat amusing—that we all agree that the United States of America is an economic powerhouse. Yet we can also just as often claim that our education system is broken. How can both be true? Creating an economic powerhouse started first by creating an education system that could matriculate highly capable workers for our country. As long as I can remember, the American ethos has been, "If you work hard and get your education, you can accomplish anything." Education has to tee 'em up, so to speak. And then from there, our graduates have to knock the ball onto the green.

There is a lot of talk about how we live in a different world today. And that our economy faces unique and new challenges. This is all true. But to say that the world has changed, therefore education is broken is unfair. It also presents a very big risk, one that I worry gets overlooked when we give into panic and resort to pointing fingers. If we say "education is broken," we are far more likely to believe we have to start over. If we start over, we are going to throw out everything that does work—*has worked*—in education. Remember that superpower our education system teed up?

Here's another example. There is a lot said about how schools today are not emphasizing "21st century skills." These skills often include things like problem solving, collaboration, critical thinking, and creativity. I smile when I hear this because I recall my teachers taking great care to teach me these skills because they were relevant back in the 20th century.

Teachers, you have always taught these fundamental skills and have always known them to be relevant to your students' future careers. That we today hear these referred to as skills pertinent only to this century validates my biggest concern about the "education is broken" or "teachers are failing" conversation: we are forgetting to look at what *works* in instruction. Instead, we are being lead to assume it's all outdated, so we have to scrap it all and start over.

Those skills have always mattered. That there's renewed attention on them is only because their need and application *have* grown more complex and broad in a computerized world.

Let's not start with education is broken. Let's start with a question: *What has changed in our world, and therefore how can education adapt?*

What has changed? We are living in a computer and machine-based world. This has put an emphasis on networks and knowledge, and it has enabled collaboration that can now span across the globe through the skilled use of technologies.

And what do educators need to do to adapt? Doesn't it seem logical that we would first start with what works? When we start with questions, we can have a conversation based on reason, rather than panic.

So, teachers, I ask you—the experts of instruction and learning. How can you take everything you know that works, everything that turned this country into a superpower, everything that pushed people like me through your fine education system and into successful careers, and then layer it with strategic, purposeful technology to bring education to the next level? If you feel you need an expert in technology to meld with your expertise in instruction, you've come to the right place.

That is one of the primary goals of this book: to help you grow comfortable merging your wisdom with strategic technology use. From this book, you will gain an understanding of why blended learning fails and why it works so that you can avoid the pitfalls of failure and plan for success. You will learn practical blended learning strategies that you can apply with ease and intention in your classroom. And you will do so from Weston Kieschnick—blended learning teacher, coach, expert, enthusiast, and evangelist. Weston has dedicated his career to students. And in today's world, that means to unlocking the most successful ways to implement blended learning in classrooms and schools so that educators may continue the tradition of education in this country: teeing students up to knock that ball onto the green of their futures.

Jaime Casap
Education Evangelist, Google

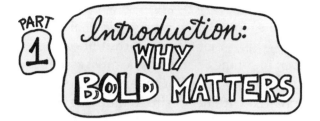

PART 1

Introduction: WHY BOLD MATTERS

Bold School, *def.*
[bohld-skool]
adjective

1. Showing the courage to hold onto old school wisdom as you blend new school technologies with purpose into instruction that *works*.

2. Daring to champion innovative technologies *and* go against the grain to stand up for old school wisdom and teacher expertise—to *finally* deliver on the promise of blended learning.

noun

3. A district, school, person, or action that embodies, personifies, breathes a *bold school* attitude, and in doing so, inspires others to do the same.

I have an affinity for blended learning. It also just so happens that I, like you, benefited immensely from masterful old school teachers. For a long time, it was difficult to reconcile these two things. Especially since I am increasingly surrounded by voices that insist embracing old school teaching will impede the success of our blended initiatives. Here's a bold statement: I reject that notion. In fact, I assert that based on thousands of classroom observations and coaching conversations, success in blended instruction is almost entirely dependent upon teachers' abilities to integrate old school wisdom that *works* with new school technologies.

Before we go further, let's address what it means to be bold. Take a look at the word. When we combine "blended" and "old," we get "bold." This is more than a fortuitous coincidence. These words happen to synthesize two of the most essential elements in a progressive educator's toolkit today. An educator's pedagogical wisdom paired with her desire to innovate will ultimately be what moves the needle for kids.

Being bold is about personifying knowledge, confidence, and courage in the face of perceived risk. It's about strength. Being bold school is my wish for you. It's why I wrote this book—so that you would have the strength of spirit, clarity of purpose, and a sense of urgency for bold actions. With that comes the blueprint for bold teaching and learning in your schools. It can be done. It has been done. It should be done.

Being bold school is not simply about replicating a methodology. It's not just about knowing a framework. It's a mindset.

Bold school educators prioritize learning and growth over hype and trend. Having great tools without great pedagogy is like buying a brand new hybrid car but never filling up the gas tank. The battery can only take the car so far. Bold schoolers don't integrate digital tools just for the sake of engagement. They blend instruction as a means of making top-notch strategies more effective and efficient than they've ever been. Engagement should be a byproduct of great instruction; it is not the main event. The main event is learning. That is our reality. We are held accountable for that reality by the seemingly never-ending tests our students take year after year. As such, we can't afford to do things that *look* effective. We have to do things that *are* effective.

Being bold school means having clarity about your strengths. Double down on those strengths and work diligently to fill in the gaps. Successful people in any field capitalize on those things that make them unique. Think about it this way: a 5'7" high school football player who plays running back and runs a 4.4-second 40-yard dash wouldn't and shouldn't try to suddenly turn himself into a great basketball player. With the right coaching, he hones his speed, quickness, and vision to become the best damn football player he can be. Why? Because that's where his greatest opportunities for athletic success live. Luciano Pavarotti didn't disregard his imposing stature and indelicate frame and try to turn himself into a prima ballerina. He doubled down on the incredible gift of his voice in order to offer the world something that aligned with his talents.

Why do we treat teachers so differently? Why would we try to take the Aristotles of our time and turn them into station rotation and flipped learning drones? This is not to say that station rotation and flipped instruction are bad. They're not. They're excellent strategies. My point is, don't hope for technology to turn you into someone you're not. Bold schoolers utilize technology to elevate their strengths while they work to develop new ones.

Courageous bold schoolers expect failure. They welcome it with open arms. They know that over the long term failing forward is better than stagnant success. Successful mediocrity at the expense of innovation and progress is bad for teachers and worse for kids. Bold school educators know it is far better for kids to improve at something they've never done than it is for teachers to be decent at the things they've always done. Try early, fail often, pursue excellence with joy, and be an omnipresent model of lifelong learning for the kids and adults around you. The world needs more learners and fewer "experts."

This book up is set up to make your learning easy and fun. The first chapter provides context on the state of blended learning today—where it's been and where it needs to go. In chapter 2, we dive deep into the Bold School Framework for Strategic Blended Learning™—a truly simple framework to reshape and guide your thinking as you implement blended instructional practices. Each chapter after that is dedicated to a high effect size instructional strategy layered with purposeful technology use to make those strategies even more impactful and make you even more excellent and effective in driving meaningful learning. Finally, for quick reference, there are Appendices that include various resources mentioned in chapters, as well as a few more that I think can be of help as you become a bold school master of blended learning. And along the way, I hope to make you laugh, think, and enjoy the process.

I hope you're excited. I hope you feel the sense of excitement I have on your behalf. You're about to embark on a journey of empowerment. The journey is not empty. It's not rhetoric. It comes with tangible strategies for success that can be implemented in classrooms tomorrow if you're bold enough to try today. Trust that I didn't write this book to feed some sense of self-importance. I wrote it because I have crystal clarity about *your* importance. Settle in. It's time to move beyond self-identifying as "old school" or "new school." It's time to be more. It's time to be *Bold School*.

CHAPTER 1 BLENDED LEARNING THAT WORKS

HOW **BOLD** SCHOOLS DO IT

I love teaching. Seriously. It's a problem. I love teaching so much that I became a teacher, I married a teacher, I host a podcast on teaching, and I author books and articles on teaching. This can only mean that my two children are destined to grow up to be . . . you guessed it! Resentful. But I won't go down without a fight.

I begin with my love for teaching because it's important to me that you understand the depth of my affinity for educators. This book is for you. It is an appreciative acknowledgment of your efforts—past, present, and future. In the spirit of that appreciation, it is also a gift. In these pages you'll find bold ideas and strategies that reflect a desire to help you design innovative learning experiences that help kids *and* preserve the sanctity of our profession. This is a road map for how to educate within the confines of a blended learning culture wrought with potholes, speed bumps, and giant walls shaped like unrealistic expectations.

I love this profession, but I wasn't always good at it. Back when I was a fresh-faced, 20-year-old college student at Iowa State, my fellow education students and I got the opportunity to do a pre-student teaching experience. It was our chance to observe masterful veteran teachers in action before being thrown in the deep end with students of our own.

Over a few weeks' time, we cycled through various classrooms at participating schools near the university, observing a number of teachers do their thing. One of these teachers was a man named Kirk Daddow, and man did he look the part. A football coach in his day, it was the greying of his brown hair and his thick mustache—not his still sturdy frame—that betrayed his age of 60 some odd years. With this man, what you saw was what you got. Even the glasses he wore couldn't obscure any animation in his expressions. If you ever found yourself wondering what he was thinking, it was because you weren't paying attention. His voice was gruff, yet captivating—perfect for holding the attention of high school students and for instilling just the right amount of fear in them when needed. There was something both theatrical and surgical about his use of words, and his voice was mesmerizing. When he spoke, it was with the sincerity of a philosopher and the authority of an expert.

As you could expect, Daddow was a master of direct instruction. Many times, all he did was lecture. If you saw this man in action, you'd know why this was often all he did; it was all he *needed* to do. He'd have his history students eating out of his hands. It didn't matter what he was lecturing about—Napoleonic Europe or laissez-faire economics—this man could make a traffic report interesting. In his classroom, the past came alive, and he always made it feel relevant to modern day. And he did this all while standing behind a podium.

Our college professor told us that if there was a particular person we wanted as our co-op teacher, we were welcome to gently broach the topic with that particular teacher. Kirk Daddow was my guy, so, I asked him if I could be his student teacher. He politely said no. He wasn't far from retirement, he said, and was in the process of scaling down, not ramping up, his workload. OK. Fair enough. But a voice in me told me not to give up. I knew I could learn so much

from him. So I did what any young, eager, shameless kid would do: I begged. And begged. And begged some more until Kirk finally relented. He was going to teach me a lesson one way or another. This was either going to be the greatest experience I could ever have . . . or the most brutal.

For the next few weeks, I watched Daddow put on his impassioned show every day. I took copious notes. I studied his every move, noted his every word choice. At the same time, I wanted to develop my own identity as a teacher. It was my aim to meld Kirk Daddow's old school expertise with my own fresh take.

The time came for me to teach my own class. Daddow asked me to do a lecture on the policies of President Teddy Roosevelt. I considered how he taught. I kept in mind what I was learning in school, particularly about different learning preferences, and I thought about how I could appeal to those. And then the light bulb went on. *I've got it*, I thought. *I'll use props to really* show *these policies.* (Master teachers reading this, I feel you cringing. And it's totally justified.)

Back at my college apartment, I scrounged around for objects that could capture an essence of Teddy Roosevelt's presidency. Bingo: a fake tree—perfect for talking about his conservation efforts. I recalled that my friend's kid brother had this cowboy on horseback figurine. That would do to explain the Rough Riders. I got super resourceful and perused the parking lot for a "big stick" (or what shaped up to be part of a tree stump) to—you guessed it—talk about big stick diplomacy. And finally, I grabbed three bed sheets because in another genius move (so much genius, I know), I decided to cover each prop for a big reveal. This was going to be awesome.

Teachers . . . we know we've tanked a lesson within about five or 10 minutes. I knew in all of five *seconds* that my first teaching experience was a disaster.

I'd gotten to the classroom early. Obviously all the props had to be well concealed beneath their sheets before the students began trickling in. The kids—if I could even call them that, just two and three years younger than I was at the time—took their seats, and I took my place at the front of the classroom. It was go time. With one dramatic move, I tore the sheet off of the fake tree and declared, "Conservation!" And with that, we were off and running . . . to Tanking Town.

A crushing panic washed over me. It was at that moment I realized I'd planned nothing beyond my brilliant props, twin sheets, and a few brief comments. No formative assessments. No pair-shares. Not even a scheduled pause in my verbal diarrhea to ask a question. I stumbled around a few thoughts on conservation before moving onto the Rough Riders. The cowboy on horseback was covered in a fitted sheet because I was a college student, and I didn't have that many sheets. As I went to "reveal" the cowboy, he got caught in the elasticized hem. Clumsily, I tried to wrestle him free as time felt like it slowed to a crawl. Once the horse was in full view, with a crack in my voice I said, "Rough Riders!" I recall muttering some random bits of information about the Rough Riders, but nothing of substance. My mind raced, desperately searching for something, anything meaningful to cut through my own uncomfortable silence.

I'm now in triage, simply trying to fill the time with anything I remembered about Teddy Roosevelt. It was painful. It was awkward. And it felt to last forever until mercifully—for all of us—the bell rang, and we were all put out of our misery.

As the kids gathered their notebooks and bags and fled the disaster zone, I placed both of my palms on the table in front of me, almost collapsing into it. As I stared down onto the table, or what felt more like the deep void that would most certainly now be my future, I felt a hand slap my back. I looked up to see a boy just barely younger than me. "Hey . . . sorry, dude," he said.

When a 17-year-old boy is offering his condolences for how severely you just embarrassed yourself, you know it's grim.

I could not bear to look at Daddow. It was not lost on me that I just tanked my first lesson in front of this masterful teacher . . . whom I had to beg to be my co-op teacher in the first place. Finally, I summoned the courage to raise my head. I saw Daddow, still sitting in the back row, arms crossed, grinning ear to ear from behind that grayed mustache. For one brief, hopeful moment, I thought, *Hey, maybe it wasn't so bad*! And then he gave me the very first piece of instructional coaching I ever got.

He looked me straight in the eyes and said, "Well. That was shit."

Ouch. It hurt. It was honest, and, worse . . . it was true.

As it turned out, Daddow wasn't just a masterful teacher; he was also a masterful coach. He sat there with me and told me what I did right (which didn't take long) and what I did wrong. We talked about why certain strategies and tools worked and why others never would. I'll never forget his overarching feedback: I placed way too much emphasis on the things, the bright shiny objects. And way too little emphasis on the instructional strategies and academic outcomes.

Sound familiar? It should. Just open the doors of aspiring blended schools across the country.

Bold School: The *Right* Way to Do Blended Learning

This is a book about blended learning—learning that comes through of a mix of traditional face-to-face instructional time and digital instructional tools. Specifically, it's about the *right* way to do blended learning—so that teachers and students alike can capture meaningful benefits and insights through technologies that support learning. What follows is based on what I've learned from 15 years of research, observation, and my own blended learning instruction experimentation and experience.

I taught my first blended learning class back in 2003, when my high school students each sat with their own laptops as we moved through my instruction. Since that time, I've studied blended learning and all the different kinds of technologies it now includes. I've worked to improve the effectiveness of technology integration in my own classroom. And now as a blended learning instructional coach, I travel the world to coach educators on the right ways to do blended learning so that it moves the needle of learner achievement.

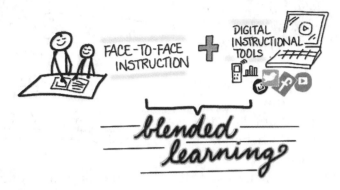

From my own experience and observing that of others, I have seen the integration of technologies into instruction make teachers more effective. Time and time again, I have witnessed technologies unlock differentiated, individualized, and personalized instruction to meet the needs of every last student in the classroom. And for as many days I've been working in education, I've seen technologies give students more control over the pace, the when, and the how of their learning so both its rigor and relevance can be elevated.

Technology is awesome. Look at all it allows us to do that we couldn't just 10, 20 years ago. In our classrooms, it gives us access to any and all information at the drop of a hat. With just a few clicks, we can get instant data about how well our students are following a lesson. And it lets our students collaborate across disciplines, across grades, across schools, even across state and country lines.

In our personal lives, technologies have allowed us to stay in much more convenient and regular touch with those important to us (and, OK, some also not so important to us). In our professional lives, technologies have brought untold amounts of efficiencies to our workdays and have made collaboration much easier.

Technology is awesome. Teachers are better. In the blended learning conversation, their role is too often left out of the equation. Any blended learning initiative that doesn't give the wisdom of teachers at least 51 percent market share will fall flat—guaranteed.

Many blended learning initiatives have fallen flat for this exact reason—that too much attention was paid to the bright, shiny technologies, and not enough attention was paid to instructional strategies, pedagogy, and academic goals that teachers apply to instruction.

To a large extent, this happened because we got a little too excited and moved a little too fast. We got excited because even as many of us are still familiarizing ourselves with educational technologies, we understand their power to improve instruction. We know that if learning is to be relevant to tomorrow's world, it has to involve technologies.

We moved too fast because we are, once again, feeling pressure to "fix" education. The pressure to correct the alleged wrongs of our education system by innovating it into something almost entirely new has been coming at us fast and furious. With the best of intentions, many of us cobbled together blended learning initiatives and rolled them out as fast as possible to reassure several constituencies. We had to get devices in our students' hands, so we did. But then what? In too many cases, we planned only to the point of putting the technologies in the classroom. You could say that when it came to this first wave of blended learning, we leapt before we looked. (Hey, at least we didn't hide the iPads under bed sheets for a grand reveal.)

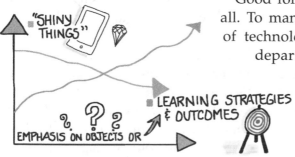

Good for you for leaping at all. To many, the introduction of technology represents the departure of everything they love about teaching. While I'm here to tell you that is beyond a shadow of a doubt not true, I'm also here to thank you. Once again, you put your students first. Once again, you attempted to adapt your instruction to fit a changing world. Once again, you embraced something beyond your comfort zone for the sake of your students. That is awesome.

I'm also here to tell you it's time to put yourselves—with all your knowledge, training, experience, and wisdom about what works in the classroom—back into the blended learning equation. We know the truth: we have to layer technologies onto our instruction. But here's another truth: we must do so with strategy, pedagogy, and purpose. That comes from educators, not from the technologies themselves.

In our haste to innovate our instruction, we threw the baby out with the bathwater. We forgot to put strategic instructional practices and purpose in front of our integration of technology. What good is innovation if it is rudderless and not built to work toward clear goals and desired academic outcomes?

It's come time for a new take on blended learning. If we want to avoid the mistakes of the first wave of blended learning, we are going to have to do something very bold.

We live in a moment where there's nonstop hype around innovation in education. And there's also incredible hyperbole around its need, with dire economic images and scenarios that lay the entire hope of our economy at the feet of teachers. We do need to adapt to the times, but this is nothing new! Educators have always had to innovate to stay relevant in a changing world. Yes, the pace of change is faster today than it has been before. But let's be clear: the challenge for us in education has been keeping up with the pace of change, not *knowing* we have to keep up with it. That so many educational leaders are coming around to more progressive educational practices and embracing innovative ideas to keep pace is great news. There's enthusiasm and support for innovation coming from many different stakeholders.

If you want to become a master of blended instruction, if you want a full-scale blended learning initiative to succeed in your school or district, you are going to have to pump the brakes on innovation. Yes, you read that right. You're going to have to slow down. And you're going to have to ask your colleagues to slow down, as well. Because moving with haste on blended learning has ended in haphazard, ineffective technology use. Instead, you're going to have to do something bold: rely on some old school expertise and latch onto the things we know unequivocally work for kids.

We are trying to track rapid change. But we shouldn't move so fast that we lose our heads—to disastrous, counterproductive results. High effect size instructional strategies are high effect size instructional strategies. Period. What works works, with or without technologies. Technologies are educational tools—critical ones, to be sure. But they themselves are not pedagogy, just as the calculator wasn't, or the typewriter before it. Technology isn't strategy. Pedagogy and goal-aligned instruction are. If we are sincere in our desire for successful blended learning, we have got to take a bold stand and stand up for old school wisdom.

Bold schools will meld blended innovation with old school wisdom—and *finally* deliver on the promise of blended learning. Bold schools will trust their educators to apply high effect size instructional strategies to technology integration—no matter how many well-intended, yet misguided people holler about a broken, outdated education system that must get flipped on its head. Bold schools will stand firm with what they know to be true.

If the notion of going against the grain of nonstop innovation hype and sky-is-falling rhetoric makes you nervous, you're not alone. It takes courage to speak up and ask people to slow down to make time for strategic thinking. In my experience, one of the most effective ways to break through the blinding power of the education "magic bullet" du jour is to zoom out and see what we're aiming for and why.

To understand why old school wisdom must be plugged back into the blended learning equation, we have to dispel some myths that are distorting the blended learning conversation and causing us to miss the mark. Then we must replace them with some new truths that will help us correct course.

Myth #1: Education is broken

I'd like to clear something up straight away: to say education is broken beyond repair is insulting. It's an insult to all those in classrooms, school offices, and district buildings working tirelessly and thanklessly to educate our children. Furthermore, this assertion is wholly inaccurate. In the 2013–14 school year, we graduated 82 percent of our high school students—our highest share of high school graduates ever (U.S. Education Department, 2015). And half of those graduates are off to college every year, also a record high (Schneider, 2016). At the same time, outcomes continue to be on the up and up. Since the 1970s, the National Assessment of Educational Progress has been monitoring student achievement of 9-, 13- and 17-year-olds. The latest results show steady and solid gains in both reading and math for 9- and 13-year-olds, as well as significant improvements in closing the achievement gap across ethnic and gender lines (National Center for Education Statistics, 2013).Things are not perfect, but we are all united in a commitment to moving the metrics of success in the right direction. And we *always* have been.

I'm a child of the 1980s and came of age in the 1990s. I remember life before digital technologies. I remember stealthily attempting to pass notes—actual pen on actual paper notes, folded ornately—in class. I remember stretching the spiral telephone cord under my bedroom door so I could talk to girls without my parents eavesdropping. I remember the mortification of mom picking up in another room and telling me it was time to go to bed.

I'd heard stories of a few people around town who had those giant cell phones that came in their own briefcases. But those were for "rich" people. When I needed to get a hold of someone, I would call that person's landline and ask the parent who answered if my friend was around. A good chunk of the time, the busy signal would greet me. Until answering machines went mainstream, the phone would often ring and ring and ring. Once cell phones got affordable and accessible, they took off like wildfire. But it would still be years before we were using T9 to send text messages. (Old school friends, please turn to the new teacher next to you and explain what T9 is.)

It wasn't until college that everyone had email addresses. Even then, we mostly used them to make social plans . . . only after we endured minutes of America Online screeching at us as it tried to make internet contact through dial-up.

My upbringing was, for the most part, analog. Yet my life today is, for the most part, digital. Now how did that happen? Based on the rhetoric around how rapidly our schools are failing because of how slowly they've been able to adapt to the digital world, you'd think I'd be sitting somewhere in the dark, probably on the fringes of society, barely able to function, much less work in the 21st century.

But I'm not. I'm typing this book on a laptop and collaborating with my editor via Google Docs in between recording and editing my podcast and blasting updates through my social media channels. After we help the kids with iPad-based homework and put them to bed, I'm kicking back with my wife in front of a movie we cue up on our Amazon Prime Video streaming service. I've managed to adapt from the analog to the digital world and thrive thanks to the education I got as a kid—long before iDevices, Tweets, and virtual clouds existed.

To say that we are failing our students because technology isn't front and center in our schools is an insult to teachers. It's an insult to my teachers. And it's an insult to all the millions of people like me who've been able to adapt in their careers as technologies have become more prevalent. We have been able to do this because of, not in spite of, our teachers.

To say we're failing our kids because we still use some strategies and tools that we used in the 20th century is just plain foolish.

It puts all the emphasis on the shiny new objects, and takes way too much emphasis off tried and true instructional strategies and pedagogy.

At its core, how is the iPad any different from the pencil? Or the typewriter? Or the calculator? Or the newspaper, for that matter? At one point, each of these technologies was new and disruptive. Just because they came along didn't mean we upended instruction as we knew it. We folded them into what was working well in our classrooms for more efficiency and effectiveness.

What is different today is the rate at which technologies are proliferating. Yes, rapid change is trickier to track. But we educators have adapted to new technologies before, and we will do it again. We just need smart guidance on smart technology integration.

When I speak about this with educators, I often use the analogy of MRI (magnetic resonance imaging) technologies found in hospitals all over the world. MRI technology is incredible. It has changed medicine by letting doctors see pictures of soft tissues inside the body with a level of detail and depth not possible with the X-ray or CT scan, and without exposing the patient to radiation. By way of this technology, doctors can make better and earlier diagnoses of certain health conditions and, in the best of scenarios, treat them before they become life threatening to the patient.

Who isn't supportive of the widespread adoption of MRI technologies in medicine?

When MRIs first came on the scene, we didn't roll the machines up to doctors' offices and say, "We've got this amazing new imaging technology we think you're really going to like. It's going to make you more effective at what you do, and it's going to get more detail about your patients' health. In turn, you're going to be able to deliver them the specific care they need to get healthy. So good luck figuring out how to use it!"

Of course we didn't do this. We didn't do this because we know that doctors need to devote their time to what they were trained to do—deliver care to patients. It's not a good use of their time to read manuals about MRI technologies and try to teach themselves the right way to use them.

Yet this is exactly what we did to teachers when it has come to digital technologies. These technologies absolutely have the power to make teachers better at what they do. They absolutely have the ability to deliver more targeted instruction to all students. But instead of providing them with purposeful, specific training about what works and what doesn't—as doctors received for the MRI—we expected them to figure it out on their own.

It would have been absurd, even dangerous, to ask doctors to figure out how to use MRI machines. And it's just as absurd, even just as dangerous, to ask teachers to figure out technologies on their own. When we take teachers away from student time, when we waste instructional classroom time on haphazard technology integration, we increase the likelihood of failing our students.

Education isn't broken. How we think about technology use and teacher training around it is.

Myth #2: The old way of teaching no longer works

Any teacher worth his or her salt has seen "Dead Poets Society." If you haven't, put this book down right now and watch it. Go on, I'll wait. Just be sure to come back.

Now wasn't that a satisfying way to spend an hour and a half? John Keating (the character played by the late, great Robin Williams) is the ultimate master of relevance. He got a classroom of awkward teenage boys to see the power of poetry, of all things. His aim wasn't to turn each of his students into future poets. His aim was to use it to teach boldness, vulnerability, and seizing the day. How does poetry relate to sports? He took them out to the field to kick soccer balls and see how both words and sports can push people to excel. How might it pertain to thinking for yourself? To the courtyard they went to simultaneously walk in as many ways as there were students. And what does poetry have to do with challenging your own perspective? Climb to the top of his desk to find out they did. He got his students to open up, think differently, imagine their futures, and dream big—all through connecting poetry to topics that mattered to them.

Can you imagine if someone went into John Keating's classroom and said, "Hey, I know you've got your students hanging on your every word. I know you've got them thinking about how what they're learning applies to the real world. And I know you're getting them to connect with their inner bold poet, see the world through a different lens, picture big futures. This is all great. But you really need to have them on iPads because iPads are where it's at right now. So please stop what you're doing and make sure you use the iPad every day for instruction."

NO captain! My captain!

This would be no different from some confused soul telling Kirk Daddow to stop with his mesmerizing lectures and instead use the horse on cowboy to make his point. And what's frightening is that I'm sure there are scores of Kirk Daddows out there being told to lecture less because lecturing is a 20th-century relic. Imagine what Daddow's students would have lost if they hadn't gotten to see this gifted man lecture? Imagine how many students out there are missing the joy and power of spellbinding direct instruction because it's so yesterday? The ironic thing is that Professor John Hattie, who is in my view one of the Patron Saints of Old School Wisdom, rates direct instruction with a .6 effect size (Hattie, 2015). That's nearly a year and a half of academic growth over one year's worth of time when implemented with fidelity. Why would we ever deem lecturing done well as anything other than bold school?

Integrating technology is a non-negotiable in the 21st-century classroom. It's also an asset—when used strategically and to elevate—not replace—instruction. But when its inclusion in learning is for no greater purpose than checking off a box or because it's the latest "hot" technology, is it really much different from a cowboy on a horse?

I'm a big believer in innovation. The world doesn't stand still, and neither should schools. Education must always adapt with the times, and this requires having big talks about innovation and what's best for students as the world evolves. But we didn't scrap everything we knew about mathematics education when the calculator came along, and we shouldn't do so now. The object is to plug technologies into high effect size instructional strategies to achieve rigorous academic outcomes.

New instructional strategies with a high effect size continue to come along, and ever more some include technologies. They are not fixed or stuck in time. Innovative thinking does lead to new strategies. But many excellent strategies have been around for decades, and we can't toss them out just because they're "old." In fact, that they've stood the test of time should show their worth, not a shelf life. Our job as educators is to keep using pedagogy that we know improves student achievement and keep an eye out for new strategies that show promise, as well. Our job is to boldly put pedagogy first, technology second.

Myth #3: Kids are digital natives

There's a great and ridiculous scene from the 2001 movie "Zoolander" where Derek Zoolander (Ben Stiller) and his male model nemesis-turned-pal, Hansel (Owen Wilson), are in a rush to prevent megalomaniac fashion designer, Jacobim Mugatu (Will Ferrell), from successfully killing the prime minister of Malaysia at the fashion show of the year. I told you it was ridiculous. Just minutes before the fashion show is set to start, investigative journalist Matilda (Christine Taylor) tells Derek and Hansel that files detailing the specifics of the sinister plot can be found on Mugatu's computer.

Derek and Hansel track down the iMac, but then they—more beauty than brains—have no idea what to do next. They've never used one of these desktop things before. They begin pressing anywhere on the computer and banging the keys, thinking this might turn it on. Perplexed by its unresponsiveness, they begin thwacking the computer with anything they can get their hands on. Seeking help, Hansel calls Matilda on his cell phone, and she tells them that the files are "in" the computer. Relief crosses his face. He bends down to peer past the candy-colored computer shell and into the guts of the iMac. "*In* the computer," he says. "It's so simple."

It's an absurd scene that, admittedly, bears no relevance to good instruction. But it does always remind me of how much we take for granted about what our students do and do not know about using technologies, particularly ones they haven't used before. It reminds me that familiarity with one kind of technology doesn't translate into familiarity with another kind of technology.

A while back, I was a helper in my son's kindergarten class. On this day, they were going to the computer lab for the very first time. Each of the 25 kids filed in and took a seat in front of a desktop, complete with a mouse. Every student—every last kid—as if on cue, went to touch the screen. Nothing happened. Minds broken. They all looked up at the teacher with big eyes, puzzled by this technology in front of them that didn't respond to touch.

There's a message out there that technology is driving a wedge between educators and students. With kids being raised on Snapchat and Virtual Reality, how could we possibly relate to them? I ask you this: what was it like for you the first time you sat in front of a computer? I bet you weren't much different from today's students when they stare down a computer for the first time. No amount of swiping can prepare them for the granddaddy of all personal computing technologies: the desktop.

Many young kids are using their parents' smartphones and tablets for entertainment and to socialize. They are skilled swipers, but this doesn't translate to computers. Nor does it translate to an ability to cultivate presentations, filter online content into fact or fiction, or engage in constructive ways online or with technologies—ways they will need to replicate in their future careers. They need you—decidedly *not* a digital native—for that.

Research backs this up. A 2015 survey of employers found that nearly 60 percent of their millennial employees (the first to have grown up on digital technologies) couldn't complete basic tasks such as sorting and searching data in a spreadsheet (Schaffhauser,

2015). While these same employees average 35 hours per week on digital media, they're honing only low-level skills that don't relate to the high-level skills needed at work.

When it comes to education, technology is the tie that binds. It is the one thing that unequivocally puts both the student and the teacher in the position of learning. Where they might be able to teach you how to navigate through a certain device's functionality, you still hold the keys when it comes to using technologies productively, smartly, and with purpose.

Myth #4: Technology must drive all decisions

Most of us are familiar with the infamous iPad rollout of the Los Angeles Unified School District. The goal of the initiative was to buy 650,000 iPads and get one into the hands of every student in the district, to the tune of about $1.3 billion (including the cost of necessary Wi-Fi upgrades). Of the many reasons blended learning initiatives can fail, the crash and burn of LA Unified's iPad initiative hit them all and should be a cautionary tale for all of us (Newcombe, 2015).

The program was criticized as being spectacularly rushed (Klein, 2014). The optics of iPads in schools mattered more than the why behind them. The goal was the technology itself, not academic outcomes. It didn't occur to enough people to ask questions about the appropriateness of iPads versus other technologies. And why would it? That is a natural question when there's a goal at hand. In the absence of goals, there's nothing to measure decisions against.

At the time, in 2012 and 2013, iPads were the hot device. The fact that they last for only a few years was overshadowed by hype and a desire for leadership to look like they were on top of fixing the district's problems. Too many believed that technology would be a magic bullet. There was too little emphasis on what problems they were trying to solve and how technologies might solve them, and too much emphasis on the bright shiny object. In the quest to hit play on iPads fast, the district did too small of a pilot program, rushed what little testing they did, and launched the official rollout with buggy educational software and weak security that students easily worked around (Gilbertson, 2014).

Another huge problem was the lack of sufficient and strategic professional development around the iPads (Kamenetz, 2013). How much training and what kind was needed for a rollout of this scale was underestimated. Teachers needed everything from iPad training, mobile device system management training, security training, and software training—and, most importantly, training on how to use iPads to advance learning goals. Most got none of this. Those who did get training got only a high-level crash course. Because the iPads themselves were the goal, training could not be targeted to coach educators on how to use iPads to meet academic achievement goals.

I don't doubt the good intentions of LA Unified's leadership. I believe they all had their students' best interests in mind. Yet the speed with which they acted led to the results you can expect when you put technology before pedagogy and strategy. With any big education initiative, it is better to slow down in the decision-making stage. If we take the time for strategic thinking and planning at the outset, not only can we avoid a lot of pain later, but we can also move more quickly through the implementation phase.

When it comes to blended learning, the bulk of the work needs to come at the start. And that work is openly and honestly discussing which technologies will elevate, not override or obstruct, strategic instruction and academic outcome goals. It is not about choosing the technologies and hoping for the best. It is about choosing the pedagogy and *planning* for the best through strategic technology decisions.

———————

Now we're clear on a few key things. Education isn't broken. Teachers aren't failing students. Technology is no magic bullet. And believing these false notions will make damn sure that we cloud rational thinking with rushed panic. That we focus on optics rather than purpose. That we demoralize our teachers and waste their time. And that we stand in the way of crafting strategic blended learning initiatives that will serve our students well and prepare them for success in their careers.

How do we get out of our own way so that we can build masterful blended learning initiatives, all pinned to big academic goals for our students and technology integration that keeps the joy in instruction *and* learning? We do this by replacing those old myths with some new truths. We do this by embracing beliefs that will lead to bold decisions at bold schools.

Truth #1: Blended learning can and should elevate, not diminish, what you do best

I often wonder what Kirk Daddow would think of blended learning. And you know what I think, honestly? He'd resist it. Initially. Because that man loved direct instruction. He loved to get students on the edge of their seats through his animated lectures. I suspect he'd see the arrival of technology as the departure of what he loved most about teaching.

But as someone who preaches *strategic* blended learning, I know he'd change his tune if I showed him the many ways technology tools could enhance what he did so brilliantly from behind his podium. (Dear Kirk Daddow, truth teller and lecture slayer: If you're reading this, first, thank you. Second, I promise I will demonstrate the power of blended learning without any silk trees or cowboys on horseback shrouded under sheets—in large part thanks to you.)

1 BLENDED LEARNING CAN & SHOULD ELEVATE WHAT YOU DO BEST

STRATEGIC BLENDING

ITEMS

• POWER
• PACE
• PERSONALIZED

I'd show him how NearPod or Google Slides would allow his students to pose questions to him in real time to avoid interrupting the lecture with a raised hand. I'd demonstrate how Kahoot! would let him joyfully and digitally engage with his students mid-lecture to make sure each was following. And for those who'd gotten lost somewhere along the line, they could ping him back to let him know they were confused, without the embarrassment of having to say so out loud in front of classmates. I'm confident that Daddow would quickly see that these technologies would create more touch points between him and his students *as* he lectured, not instead of it. He'd get that technologies could help him clarify as needed to make sure every last student in his classroom was with him. And because Daddow cared so much about his students, I believe he would embrace any and all tools that let him continue to lecture with that much more differentiation, individualization, and personalization.

I have full faith that Daddow would quickly realize that when strategically implemented, blended learning has the power to reach more students by accommodating different learning styles and paces, accelerating learning by delivering personalized instruction, increasing the amount of data available to him on all of his students' progress, and allowing students to access diverse learning materials both in and out of school (U.S. Department of Education: Use of Technology in Teaching and Learning, n.d.). All while allowing him to double down on what he did best.

It's time we look at our teachers and ask, *What do you do awesomely? What do you love most about teaching?* You're a master of peer tutoring? OK, perfect. Now let's find you the technology tool that improves your ability to match partners based on needs and abilities, and track progress. Cooperative learning is the reason you get out of bed each morning? Great, let's get you doing more of that, with more data and the more informed decisions that data enables.

When the expertise and wisdom of the teacher is given equal weight in the blended learning equation, *that* is bold school. It is bold because instead of steamrolling educators with technology and squeezing what they do best out of instruction, the teacher gets to choose the technologies that make her better and more efficient at what she loves to do.

Truth #2: Instructional practices, pedagogy, and academic outcomes must drive technology decisions

Studying the trials and tribulations of LA Unified's iPad initiative shows the colossal risks of starting first with a technology. Instead, successful blended learning starts with the academic outcomes you hope students achieve through your instruction and the instructional strategies that will help get them there (Okojie, M., Olinzock, A. A., & Okojie-Boulder, T. C., 2006). Then and only then do you start looking at the different technology options that make sense.

To work, technology integration has to be strategic. Strategic technology use is use that is purposefully chosen for its ability to move you toward defined student learning goals. When technology isn't rooted in pedagogy and hasn't been vetted and tested for its ability to help your students reach learning objectives, then its use is haphazard; this is the opposite of strategic. It's like putting up the sail without pointing it in the direction you want to boat to go. Or worse, without even knowing where you want to go and why.

Strategic technology integration is technology integra-

2 INSTRUCTIONAL PRACTICES, PEDAGOGY, & ACADEMIC OUTCOMES MUST DRIVE TECHNOLOGY DECISIONS

GOALS
OUTCOMES
① OUTCOME
② STRATEGY
③ TECHNOLOGY

tion that relies on high effect size instructional strategies. What this means is that teachers first decide the effective instructional strategy, and then work the technological tool into it. This is that old school wisdom—the experience and expertise of educators. We know what works in the classroom. We cannot throw it all out just to make room for technologies. We did that in the first wave of blended learning. For this next wave of blended learning, we must be bold school and hold tight to our old school wisdom and let it guide technology decisions.

Bold schools have the courage to keep pedagogy the number one priority. Bold schools don't kowtow to pressure to get devices in hands *fast* just for the optics of it. Bold schools get devices in hands once their strategic purpose is identified, broadcasted, and known.

Truth #3: Becoming a blended learning master means knowing how to use technologies to move toward academic goals

Just as blended learning initiatives have got to be strategic and born from pedagogy, so too must the training around them. Imagine if I asked you to teach me how to cook an egg and said nothing more. An egg can be fried, boiled, scrambled, or poached. Each way of cooking it requires different tools and ingredients. To tell you to teach me how to cook an egg isn't enough.

Now what if I asked you to train me how to use laptops in instruction. We can use a laptop for dozens of educational purposes. We can use it to make a spreadsheet. Or send an email. Or work in Google Docs. Or look up online how to build a suspension bridge. Or listen to different kinds of classical music. Or edit a film. Or write an essay.

Research has shown that merely training teachers on how to use a technology in a technical sense or for one application will ensure that they keep a narrow view of blended learning (Okojie, et al., 2006). Meaning, this kind of narrow training tends to cause teachers to believe that technologies are tools to help them teach, not help students learn. Training from this place will all but guarantee that blended learning initiatives will fail. Instead, technology training has got to be pinned to pedagogy and learning goals if we are to have any hope of successful blended instruction. How we get technology training must be driven by our specific goals. Otherwise, the training will flail about, be irrelevant, confuse teachers, and waste everyone's time.

The goals of our blended learning must be clear. And then professional development around them has to be designed according to those goals.

We cannot put technologies in front of teachers and expect they'll figure it out. And if we do make that mistake, we cannot blame them if blended learning initiatives fail. Teachers are not IT employees and data analysts. They're teachers. Their purpose in school is to work with students, cultivate relationships, and deliver targeted instruction that helps all students learn. Their purpose is to teach students, not teach themselves new technologies.

Remember: we wouldn't expect doctors to teach themselves how to use MRI machines and then blame them when they made mistakes. We cannot do the same to teachers attempting to use technology in the classroom.

We know that we have to roll out successful blended learning initiatives. From now on, we're going to be bold school and put teachers and their wisdom back in the equation. Blended learning can only be successful if we let teachers use technology with intention and strategy. This also means it can only be successful if teachers get the technical *and* pedagogical training they need to know how to use technologies to this end. Bold schools provide professional development on strategic blended learning for *all* teachers so that they will become blended learning masters.

Truth #4: You are still the smartest, most needed person in the room

Using technologies for the first time can be a little scary. I know, I get it. They can be that much scarier when there's all this pressure to get them in your classrooms fast. And when you feel your students, with fewer years on earth and less experience than you, can navigate them much quicker than you can, well, that fear factor keeps climbing. It is a surreal experience when a young student makes you feel like they're smarter than you. Yet in the digital age, all educators have had this experience at least once.

Since the dawn of the one-room schoolhouse, teachers have been the smartest person in the room. All these devices and social media platforms are undermining this long-held authority. Or at least making us feel that way. I'm sure some of us have seen 5-year-olds figure out certain things on an iPad faster than most adults ever could.

But that 5-year-old doesn't yet know how to use iPads or Chromebooks to collaborate with others to create a podcast. He doesn't know how to tell fake from real information when researching or reading online. Nor does he know how to use apps to collect data, run an analysis, and turn that information into targeted instruction. He also can't initiate a multi-person video meeting to discuss the launch of a new product and how best to market it in Europe, Asia, and North America. And he definitely doesn't know that what we do and say online can follow us for our entire lives and that we have to consider the consequences every time we go online.

Only an adult can teach him all these things. And that's you. You are still the smartest person in your classroom.

There's also a fear that technology will replace the need for teachers. Or at least cut into a good amount of face-to-face student-teacher time.

Powerful instruction has always been and will always be about relationships. Relationship is the universal language of resonance. Yeah, kids love their devices. They love to use them to socialize with friends and entertain themselves. But if you think using a technology to bond with a student will work, you are wrong. Don't believe me? Just try it. Resonance isn't built on technology. Nor is it built in liking the same things as your students. Resonance is built on trust and caring. Only once a student knows you authentically care about her and her success can a relationship take shape.

If you want a rigorous and relevant classroom, you have to cultivate relationships with all your students. When they know you have their best interests at heart, they will trust you. They will listen when you talk, and they will want to do well for and by you. They will engage in your instruction because they believe you when you say it matters for their futures. And they will rise to meet the rigorous expectations you set for them because your relationship proves you believe in them.

Only you can do this. A computer will never be able to replace the caring relationship and mutually respectful authority you can establish with each of your students.

———

Your old school wisdom is irreplaceable. And by now, I hope you believe it's also indispensable to something else: your successful, bold school blended learning plans.

CHAPTER 2

A FRAMEWORK for BOLD SCHOOL

B old school is an attitude. It's a mindset. It's a way of thinking and behaving.

Bold school is a space we all must inhabit so that all of our thinking, decisions, and instruction come from a place of purpose. And that is a place where you keep yourself—with all your wisdom, experience, and expertise—in the equation as you confidently meld what works in instruction with technology tools, both methodically and with purpose. Bold schools give you and your teams the space and time to frontload the work of innovating classrooms with thorough thinking and planning. You start first with the academic outcomes you hope to achieve, then move to devising the strategy or strategies that will realize those academic outcomes. And then and only then do you decide the technology tools that make the most sense for the strategy. Bold schools and bold school educators do not start with the technology for technology's sake, nor do they get devices in hands as fast as possible for empty optics.

The point of this chapter is to help you get into the bold school headspace, to help you inhabit that attitude and methodology of the bold school educator and leader, and to help prime your brain for boldness. I've coached teachers in every corner of this country to develop this process. It's easier than it sounds. I know it has to be.

27

I've sat in your seat many times as a classroom teacher. I know that if an "expert" offers me a plan that takes more time to design than it does to deliver, my likelihood of implementing that plan decreases with every minute it adds to my planning. Adding more to your plate is not my intention. In fact, I intend to do the opposite. I want to impart a design methodology that allows you to plan less and do more for kids. When the final bell rings, I want you to leave the building feeling less exhausted and more satisfied that you've moved kids along the proficiency spectrum. I want kids to leave feeling less jittery from a day of sitting and more curious from a day of being immersed in powerful learning.

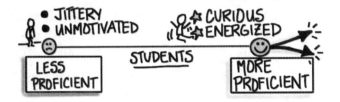

After designing, delivering, observing, and coaching thousands of blended lessons, I've devised a five-step framework to move you toward becoming a bold school educator.

It's a framework to help you think through your goal, strategy, tools, and self-assessment process as you approach and implement any blended learning initiative or instructional plan. Make this framework habit, and you are certain to embody bold school. From this place, you will launch successful blended learning initiatives and use blended learning instructional practices that *work*.

First, however, we need a quick course on the differences between goals, strategies, and tools. In grasping these differences, you will see why this is where we have to start.

The Goal → Strategy → Tool Paradigm

This goal-strategy-tool paradigm is all around us. It's in business. It's in sports. It's in budgeting. It's in cooking Thanksgiving dinner. It's everywhere. Most of us know this paradigm merely by living; we know it intuitively, but most, I have found, don't know it technically. When we don't know it technically, we won't always know how to apply it successfully. Furthermore, the words often get misused and confused.

Learning this paradigm and, importantly, the difference between goals, strategies, and tools, is taught in every business school (however, in business, the word tactics is typically used in place of tools). Yet for all its applications and power, it should be taught in *all* schools.

Just as effective, smart use of this paradigm can drive profits, market share, and general success in business, in education it can drive reaching desired academic outcomes, improving both instruction and student learning, and boosting overall student growth and success. Just as this model allows employees to make decisions and act on firmer business ground, it ensures educators make decisions and act on firmer pedagogical ground.

Let's get technical for a minute about this paradigm because in its presence, the game can get changed. In its absence, sometimes we get lucky and things just work out for the best. But in most cases, without first starting with the goal, then choosing the strategy and then the tools accordingly, initiatives and plans are left to be leaves in the wind. They will be at the mercy of a disorganized process, differing opinions, and moving goal posts. If the plans land anywhere at all, who knows where they'll land and to what effect.

The Goal → Strategy → Tool Paradigm Defined	
Goal	The _result_ you want to achieve.
Strategy	The plan for _how_ you will achieve this goal.
Tools	_What_ you will use and apply to achieve the goal associated with the strategy.

OK, I realize this might still feel a bit abstract. This paradigm is one of those things better learned through example than through definition. So let's turn to Beetlejuice.

Example 1: Beetlejuice

Ahh, Beetlejuice, the Father of Modern Strategy. Kidding. I'm pretty sure that guy was from Harvard, not a Tim Burton film. But a Tim Burton film is, I think, a much more fun way to learn this.

In "Beetlejuice," a young couple (Barbara, played by Geena Davis, and Adam, played by Alec Baldwin) drives their car off a bridge, and both drown in the water below. However, they don't know they've died, as their ghosts carry on and look as they did when they were alive. It's not until they get home that Barbara sees no reflection in a mirror and they discover the *Handbook for the Recently Deceased* that they begin to think that they are, in fact, deceased themselves.

Time passes. They meet Beetlejuice (played by Michael Keaton). They encounter sand monsters. They discover bureaucracies exist in the Netherworld, suggesting even death will not liberate us from red tape. And eventually their house gets sold to the eccentric Deetz family (whose daughter is played by Winona Ryder in all her Gen X, angsty teen glory). Barbara and Adam decide they must somehow get this family to move out of what they still believe is their home. So they devise a plan to do just that. They agree that they will make the most of their new found dead-ness and "haunt" the house, with the hope of scaring the Deetz family away.

Let's consider Barbara and Adam's process through the paradigm:

Goal: Get their house back.

Strategy: Scare the new tenants so much that they decide to move out.

Tools: Make scary ghost noises, clank chains, shapeshift into monsters . . . the usual.

Is it beginning to make sense? Let's try a couple more, just to make sure this really sinks in and begins to prime your brain for bold school.

Example 2: Train to run a half marathon in six months

Let's say you want to run a half marathon in six months. You've never been a serious runner, so you will need a training plan:

Goal: Run a half marathon six months from now.

Strategy: Use a mix of nutrition and training to build endurance.

Tools: You will run on the treadmill at your gym three times a week. You will start running for 20 minutes each trip to the gym, and then every two weeks, you will add five more minutes to your running time. You will weight train once a week to strengthen muscles. You will make sure you get the suggested amount of protein for every meal. As your training progresses, you will gradually add in more carbohydrates to power your longer-distance runs. And you will track your water intake every day to maintain hydration.

Example 3: Train to run a half marathon in six months—in under two hours

Now let's look at how the strategy and tools shift when goals change. Imagine you want to run the same half marathon, except in this scenario, you want to cross the finish line in under two hours. You're still pretty new to regular running, so here's your plan:

Goal: In six months from now, complete a half marathon in under two hours.

Strategy: Use a mix of nutrition and training to build both endurance and speed.

Tools: You will run on the treadmill three times a week, adding five more minutes to time your running time every two weeks for the first three months. For the final three months, you will add five minutes to your running time every week. You will use sprint interval training (short bursts of sprinting) on the treadmill to build up capacity for speed. You will do weight lifting training two times a week to build muscle strength for speed. In the first session, you will focus on upper body and core strength training, and in the second session, you will focus on lower body and core strength training. As far as diet, you will make sure you eat the recommended amount of protein in every meal. You will increase your carbohydrate intake as your training progresses to fuel your longer runs. And you will track your water intake to make sure you don't get dehydrated.

Notice how important it is to be specific in your goals, as this has implications on the strategy and the tools you select. There's an acronym many of you are aware of to help you devise the kind of goals that will set you up for a successful strategy: SMART. SMART goals are those that are Specific, Measureable, Achievable, Relevant, and Time bound.

Not only does this paradigm greatly help increase the odds you will achieve a desired goal, it allows you to check your progress. This is because you have a goal against which to measure your decisions and progress. In the half marathon example, one month into your training, you can ask yourself if the strategy is working. You can check in again a month later and assess if you are making meaningful improvements in your ability to run for longer differences.

If you aren't improving, you can evaluate your chosen tools. Perhaps you'll find you're not eating enough carbohydrates. Perhaps you'll find you need to weight lift more frequently. Perhaps you'll find you're training too much. Sometimes a new tool needs to be swapped out for an old one. Sometimes you might even find that the strategy isn't quite right and that it needs an overhaul. Just keep in mind that any time a strategy changes, all the tools need a second look to make sure they match the new strategy. In many cases, they no longer will, so they must be replaced with those that do.

If you want to feel super smart, in the business world, these checks are put in place in advance and called objectives. They are, in short, mini goals that will move a company closer to the goal in a methodical and measurable way. If you're meeting your goal-aligned objectives, you are, in theory, using the right strategy and the right tactics. If you're not, the accuracy and relevance of the objectives should be checked. The strategy in place should be questioned, and the appropriateness of the tools should be reconsidered. In doing an audit of the overall paradigm, hopefully the issue will reveal itself, and the fix can be determined. Then it all starts over again. If you're serious about achieving a goal, its progress and all inputs need to be regularly assessed. Otherwise, little mistakes can spiral into massive errors.

Peter Drucker is commonly called the Father of Modern Management. One way or another, he's responsible for the lion's share of management theory out there today. He was a big believer in strategic planning, both in general and in management. He is often quoted as rightly saying, "What gets measured gets improved."

A few years ago, I was at a conference where we were talking about why plans fail or succeed. The speaker put up a chart to capture the difference between strategic plans and non-strategic plans (those leaves in the wind that sometimes get lucky and land on success, but in most cases fall aimlessly into failure). I cannot find this genius little chart, so I will attempt to rebuild it for you. But please keep in mind this was not originally my creation:

	NOT STRATEGIC	STRATEGIC
	Don't Know Why	*Know Why*
Success	I succeeded, but I don't know why.	I succeeded, and I know why.
Failure	I failed, but I don't know why.	I failed, and I know why.

I love this chart for a couple of reasons. One, it embodies the difference between having and lacking a strategy. When you are strategic, you can retrace—forward and backward—steps and progress *toward* a goal. Two, it embodies the reality of having a strategy. When you are strategic, you can also retrace—forward and backward—steps and progress *away* from a goal. Strategic or not, we're still human beings. Being strategic greatly improves the odds of success—but it doesn't guarantee it. What it does all but guarantee is that when our strategic plans get off track or even fail, there will be all this great, helpful, informative data baked in. You will be able to pinpoint where things went wrong, why, and to what effect.

Upon completion of any plan, strategic or otherwise, it's wise to do a post-mortem, where stakeholders discuss why something went well or didn't go so well. When you are strategic, you will be able to get to the why. When you are not strategic, you won't be able to understand with confidence why you succeeded (making it difficult to replicate this success again) or why you failed (making it difficult to avoid failure next time).

I hope by now this is all starting to crystallize in your brain. As a brief paradigm recap, if we want to make any sort of change or improvement or launch a new program, we start with the desired goal, and a SMART one at that. Then we determine an effective strategy for that goal. Only then do we figure out the tools that make the most sense for that strategy. As you've seen, there can be more than one tool for a strategy. (And for big goals, there can be more than one strategy.)

Now you're ready to think about the goal-strategy-tool paradigm in terms of blended learning.

But first, a final note on how these words are used—and often misused. To be strategic—think strategically, act strategically, make strategic decisions—means to do something that encompasses all three parts of this paradigm. It means there's a clear

"IF ONE COMPONENT IS MISSING, SOMETHING IS NOT AND CANNOT BE STRATEGIC."

goal, there's a plan in place to achieve that specific goal, and tools and tactics are chosen to serve that plan. If one component is missing, something is not and cannot be strategic. I'd like to put a bee in your brain about this. Every time you hear the word "strategic" or "strategy," check its use. Is it being used correctly? Is it being confused for tactics, tools, and techniques? (I think you will soon learn odds are high it is.) Is there an opportunity or a need to correct a misconception about strategy so that you can help others improve the odds of realizing their goals? Or perhaps even define that goal in the first place?

If we are to serve our students best, we must also serve our colleagues in helping them understand this paradigm. To that end, I have a suggestion: if a coworker says that her strategy is a graphic organizer or a rubric, gently and patiently correct her. Point out that's a tool, and potentially an excellent one—so long as it's linked to a strategy and a goal.

When it comes to making strategic plans, the words we use matter, as does how we use them.

The Bold School Framework for Strategic Blended Learning™

How many times have you started or seen your colleagues start a blended learning initiative or instructional practice with the digital device—the tool? I'll tell you how many times I've seen this: *most* of the time. In fact, I'd venture a guess that you, yes, even you, have at one time or another started planning a lesson by asking yourself the wrong question. It probably sounded something like, "How am I going to use Chromebooks today?" Or, "I'm being observed next week; what do I want my kids to do with the iPads?"

But we have a bee in our brains now. A bold school bee, if you will. And we're not going to do that anymore. Nor are we going to stand by while others do this anymore. Instead, we're going to apply the Bold School Framework for Strategic Blended Learning and encourage others to do the same.

This framework is not a lesson design template. Lord knows you don't need another one of those to fill out. You can apply the framework to any instructional design frame or technological device. It's lesson plan and device agnostic. This is because it's not about the instructional plan or device. It's about the goal, and the framework helps you pull in the instructional plan and device(s) that will best serve the goal.

The Bold School Framework for Strategic Blended Learning is a thinking process. It's metacognitive more than tangible. It was designed to help shape your thinking so that you craft pedagogically-based, bold school blended learning initiatives and instructional plans that increase teacher effectiveness and improve student outcomes. In schools that have adopted the Bold School Framework, teachers are finally delivering on the promise of blended learning.

The Bold School Framework for Strategic Blended Learning™

OVERVIEW	
Step 1	Identify Desired Academic Outcome(s)
Step 2	Select a Goal-Aligned Instructional Strategy That *Works*
Step 3	Choose Digital Tool(s)
Step 4	Plan Blended Instruction
Step 5	Self-Assess Your Plans and Progress with a Framework

Step 1: Identify Desired Academic Outcome(s)

What was true in our old schools is still true in our new schools: we are held accountable for students' academic achievement. As such, it's not enough to do what's new, or what's exciting, or what's cool. (Are people still using "cool"? Whatever—I am. I guess that's the "old school" talking.) We have to do what needs to be done to help students achieve at the highest levels. This requires that we start first with the desired academic goal, the *result* we hope to achieve or the skill we seek to cultivate. You do this by asking questions relevant to the task at hand. If it's a school-wide blended learning initiative, you might ask, *What are the academic outcomes we hope to achieve through a blended learning program?* If the task is planning a learning series, you might ask, *What specific skills do I want my students to develop?* Note that it is possible to have more than one academic goal, but it is not always necessary.

Ideally, these skills and desired academic outcomes will be aligned to whatever your school or district has decided are the priority standards. And ideally, these priority standards are aligned to an overall school or district improvement plan. Why? You know this . . . because then everything—all conversations, considerations, and decisions—is aligned to goals. Then it's *strategic*. We're linking both the macro—what happens in our classrooms—to the micro—the academic and learning priorities of the district or school. Strategic! You're getting it . . .

Step 2: Select a Goal-Aligned Instructional Strategy That Works

Now that you know what you hope your students learn or gain, you can choose the instructional strategy, or strategies— the *how*—that is designed to achieve that learning goal. Keep in mind that because we are going for bold school blended learning here—where we meld our wisdom about what works in the classroom with technologies—you are only choosing from instructional strategies that you know work. In many cases, you might find more than one works, so you can choose from among them or, where it won't become clunky, use more than one strategy in pursuit of an academic goal. What matters most is that you make sure your instructional strategy menu is filled with options that have a high effect size and have shown to move the needle in student learning.

The question to ask at this point is, *Which instructional strategy that works will best help my students meet the desired academic outcome?*

As an example, let's say your desired outcome is to teach children to determine the main idea of a text, recount the key details, and explain how they support the main idea. What is a proven instructional strategy that will move students toward this goal? One instructional strategy that would make sense here is reciprocal teaching. It is a strategy that has proven to *work*. It has a high effect size, and it also links directly to your goal.

I know what you might be thinking. Reciprocal teaching can be traced back to Lev Vygotsky, a man born in 1896. It's an old, uncool, and unequivocally 20th-century approach. Yep, it is! But it works, so who cares? When kids have the opportunity to predict, clarify, question, and summarize, they learn! It may not be flashy, but it's sure as hell effective. Besides, watch what happens when we use technology to elevate this old school strategy. You won't believe how deep we can dive.

Learning is King. Growth is Queen. "Cool" is the court jester. The jester is technology. And the jester has value, but don't put him in charge of the kingdom.

On a related note, now that computer and internet technologies have been around for a while, there are new instructional strategies that have technology built into them. An example is interactive video, with a .54 effect size (Hattie, 2015). If you choose a technology-based instructional strategy, just be sure that it's been around long enough to have been studied and deemed effective.

Once you have a bold school instructional strategy in place, then and only then do we move onto the digital tools.

Step 3: Choose Digital Tool(s)

See, I didn't even need to phrase this step about *what* we'll use to achieve the goal as "Select the Digital Tool or Tools That Will Support Your Strategy." Because now you know, in a technical sense, what it means for something to be strategic. And you know that we are being strategic using this framework. Your bold school brain is taking shape.

Now it's time to ask, *Which digital tool or tools will help elevate the strategy and be most effective and efficient in meeting the outcome?* Asking this question in this order—the bold school order, if you will—is the goose that lays the golden egg when it comes to blended learning. In using this thinking framework to arrive at a strategic blended learning plan, you are infinitely more likely to finally deliver on the promise of blended learning. This will make sure you arrive at a blended learning initiative or lesson plan that is going to allow students to simultaneously learn and gain practical technology skills. Why? Because you've just melded your old school wisdom—instructional strategies that work—with technology use that has a specific, relevant purpose. You arrived at blended learning with purpose, pedagogy, and strategy. You arrived at bold school.

In doing so, you've also avoided one of the most common pitfalls that cause so many blended learning initiatives to disappoint. You didn't create an account in Google Classroom and then ask what you should do with it. You figured out what you needed to do to get your students working toward a specific learning goal, and then you sought out Classroom *because* you determined it was a strategic tool that could help you meet your goal.

A final note about bold school technology use: start slowly. Just because you're going to teach a blended class doesn't mean you need to throw the technology kitchen sink at it. While it's not uncommon for multiple tools to be capable of advancing a strategic plan, it's usually also not necessary. Start with one tool. Familiarize yourself and your students with it. Once everyone is comfortable with the technology and learning goals are being met, experiment with adding in another tool if it makes strategic sense. What you want to avoid is overwhelming your kids (and yourself) with so many new technologies at once that everyone ends up devoting most of their time learning the tool, not the academic concept. Slow, steady, and strategic wins the race here.

Step 4: Plan Blended Instruction

Now that your strategy is in place and you've selected tools that will advance that strategy as you help your students achieve a specific academic outcome, you can plan your class. What gets planned gets done. What doesn't get planned might not get done and is left to chance. We're bold school, and we're here for our students' futures, so we aren't going to leave anything to chance. When you write down how the class will unfold, you can make certain you're including the rigorous thinking exercises and relevant application of new skills that will get your students to that academic outcome.

Step 5: Self-Assess Your Plans and Progress with a Framework

We're not quite done. We need to check the viability of our blended learning initiative or instructional plans at the outset and throughout implementation. This is what we—people committed to preparing our students for success in their careers—do.

Being strategic greatly improves the odds of reaching our desired goals. However, we're still human, and some bumps in the road are inevitable. After all, we are blending old school wisdom with new technologies. Anytime we're dealing with new and changing technologies, there will be unknowns and kinks to work out. Anytime we launch a new initiative or plan, there will be kinks to work out. This is OK. Innovation has to leave room for error if there is to be any hope of its ultimate success. What matters is putting in checks to find these errors before they derail success. This entire five-step framework is designed to avoid mistakes from spinning out of control to the point of failure. This last step is the ultimate insurance policy: it will ensure mistakes do not go unnoticed.

Find a self-assessment framework you like and understand, and then use it with fidelity to check your initiatives and plans. Use the framework to vet your plans for effectiveness at the outset, and then keep using it to check progress toward goals throughout implementation. Let these frameworks give you insight into the potential impact of an initiative or plan, as well as inform you when you need to correct course with a new strategy or tool once you've started.

When it comes to blended learning, many people's assessment go-to is SAMR—the **S**ubstitution, **A**ugmentation, **M**odification, **R**edefinition Model, developed by Dr. Ruben Puentedura. The SAMR Model was groundbreaking in certain ways. It helped a lot of people think about their technology use in instruction with more complexity and care. That alone makes it valuable for the conversations it started. It is also of the moment, hip, cool. Sound familiar?

We're bold school, so we don't let hip and cool drive our decisions. We stand up for what works and point out what doesn't work—even if it means going against the grain. In that spirit I will say this: the SAMR Model can be useful in helping you determine how innovative your use of technology is in learning tasks. But it cannot help you determine how rigorous or relevant the learning and thinking are behind that task; nowhere does it mention student learning. In SAMR, tech is king. For that reason, it is insufficient. In many ways, SAMR is akin to a tech tool: cool! But its value is possible only if it's first aligned strategically to a goal.

For this reason, I recommend the more robust and student-centric Rigor/Relevance Framework® to vet your blended learning plans (Daggett, 2016). The Rigor/Relevance Framework is a powerful tool to consider how rigorous a plan is, as well as how relevant it is to the real world. The Framework is built upon two continuums. The vertical axis, the Knowledge Taxonomy, pertains to levels of rigor and is derived from Bloom's Revised Taxonomy. The horizontal axis, the Application Model—developed by the International Center for Leadership in Education—pertains to how knowledge is put to use and to what degree of complexity and relevance to the world beyond school.

Together, the two continuums make up four quadrants: Quadrants A, B, C, and D. In Quadrant A, a plan or goal is of low rigor and low relevance, meaning the rigor of the thinking is low. The plan will not demand from the student high levels of cognition, nor will it have much relevance beyond one discipline or the classroom. In Quadrant B, we've pushed the relevance further along the application continuum, meaning it can apply to more disciplines or the world beyond school, but rigor has not increased. In Quadrant C, we've done the opposite; we've increased the rigor of a task, or the complexity of thinking required to complete it, but have not improved the relevance of it to the real world. In Quadrant D, a task or plan is both sufficiently rigorous and relevant. It demands high-level cognition and its application is broad in that extends to multiple disciplines and the real world (e.g., careers), even including to unpredictable, real-world situations. When we're closing in on Quadrant D learning, students are using the complex levels of cognition they will need in their careers *and* they also understand that their time in school is 100 percent relevant to those future careers.

Rigor/Relevance Framework®

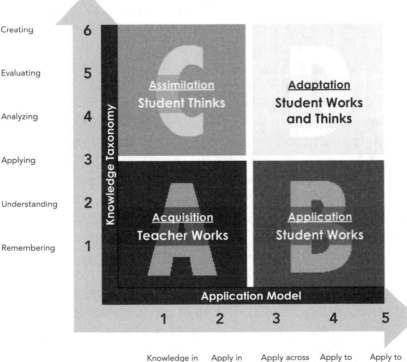

While Quadrant D is the goal, it's important to keep in mind that it's not going to be possible, or even the most effective objective, every time—particularly where scaffolding is a smart instructional strategy. When we scaffold, by definition we are not starting in Quadrant D; we're building up to it. When using the Rigor/Relevance Framework as your self-assessment tool, keep objectives—those mini goals in service of the big goal—in mind. Work toward Quadrant D. Aim to get there. But move up through the quadrants as needed. And you are bold school; you know when scaffolding toward goals is an appropriate strategy. You are also self-assessing, so you know when mini goals have been met and you and your students are ready to graduate to another quadrant.

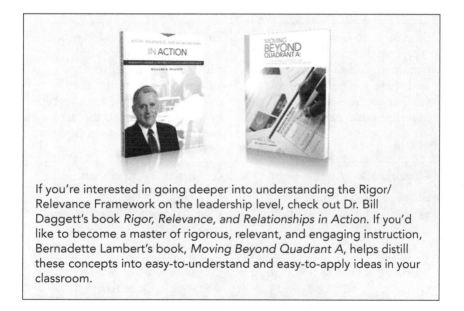

If you're interested in going deeper into understanding the Rigor/ Relevance Framework on the leadership level, check out Dr. Bill Daggett's book *Rigor, Relevance, and Relationships in Action*. If you'd like to become a master of rigorous, relevant, and engaging instruction, Bernadette Lambert's book, *Moving Beyond Quadrant A*, helps distill these concepts into easy-to-understand and easy-to-apply ideas in your classroom.

The uses for the Rigor/Relevance Framework are broad. It can be used to think through something as big as an entire learning initiative or as small as one learning task. It's a simple, but powerful tool. And it was designed to allow for the same thinking approach to be used to whatever it is you are trying to assess for both rigor and relevance. No less, let's get familiar with using the

Rigor/Relevance Framework as a technology vetting and assessment tool through an example.

Using G Suite for Education (formerly Google Apps for Education) in a Reading Task

Academic Outcomes: Determine the central idea of a text. Provide an objective summary.	
Quadrant C—Assimilation: *Students extend and refine acquired knowledge to automatically and routinely analyze information, solve problems, and create unique solutions.*	**Quadrant D—Adaptation:** *Students think with complexity and apply knowledge and skills to unpredictable situations.*
Students use Google Slides to storyboard essential elements from text. Slides include photo and video elements collected via Google Search to support assertions and conclusions.	Students use Google Hangout to debate text assertions with peers in other regions. Summaries, prompts, and essential questions are created by students prior to the activity and provided to all via Google Classroom.
Quadrant A—Acquisition: *Student tasks require simple recall and basic understanding of knowledge.*	**Quadrant B—Application:** *Students use acquired knowledge to solve problems, design solutions, and complete work.*
Students access text via Google Classroom and close read for comprehension. They type responses to short answer comprehension questions, name the file, and submit it to the teacher.	Students work in teams via Google Docs to create collaborative Cornell Notes to summarize text. Teams peer review and provide feedback via comments in Google+.

Notice that in Quad D, technology is used to elevate learning. In this situation, the technology opens up new doors, while keeping learning goals the number one priority.

Let's return to the SAMR Model. If you are comfortable and attached to this model—great. Another priority of bold school is enhancing what you do and enjoy in instruction, not taking it away from you. To enhance SAMR, it should be used as an overlay to the Rigor/Relevance Framework. This way, you can determine for sure that you are applying technologies with an eye both on innovative use *and* student-centric instruction.

Again, as I briefly mentioned, SAMR stands for **S**ubstitution, **A**ugmentation, **M**odification, and **R**edefinition. Let's break it down.

> **Substitution:** The technology trades in one tool for another to complete a task exactly as it would have been approached before computers.
>
> **Augmentation:** The technology allows students to complete a common task in an effective way through some new functionality.
>
> **Modification:** The technology tool offers some new possibilities as to how to complete parts of a task.
>
> **Redefinition:** The technology use allows students to complete a task entirely in ways once not possible without computers.

When we view the SAMR Model in combination with the Rigor/Relevance Framework, we can see that Substitution is Quad A, and Augmentation is Quad C. While Augmentation is asking more complex thinking of students, neither of these achieves relevance. Modification is Quad B, which means now our technology use is getting more relevant to how students will need to use it in the real world, which is a goal of our technology use in general. This is good progress. Finally, Redefinition is Quad D. Now we're asking kids to use technologies in a way that allows them to think deeply and in real-world circumstances not possible without technologies. Ding ding ding! But keep in mind: we're overlaying SAMR onto the Rigor/Relevance Framework. Be sure that your technology use is supported by thinking and knowledge application that are of high rigor and relevance, respectively, to secure that Quad D learning.

Rigor/Relevance Framework® and SAMR

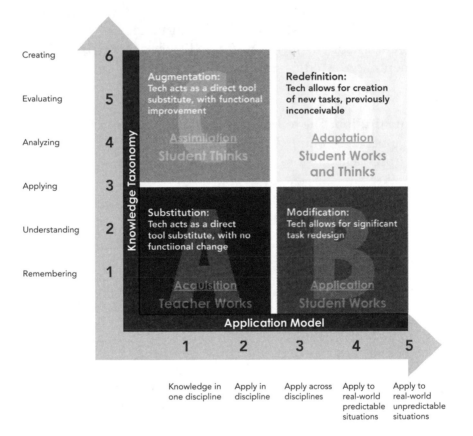

Self assess—at the outset and throughout. And you will be well on your way to bold school blended learning—blended learning that *works*.

You know why blended learning must be infused with bold school thinking. You know why it's time for a new and improved, strategic take on blended learning, and you know what to do to avoid past mistakes. You know how to approach all blended learning initiatives and plans so that they're built for success. You've got a bold framework to do so, one that is gradually changing your brain by making a habit of strategic thinking and planning. Grasping this full context of blended learning is half the battle, and the half that is most commonly missing in today's blended learning.

Each of the following chapters highlights a specific blended learning instructional strategy so that you can apply it in your own classroom, and each uses the Bold School Framework for Strategic Blended Learning. (See the end of this chapter for a version of the framework that can serve as a guide.) You will now read these strategies from a different headspace. You will notice that they make more sense, as you will see how cohesive they are, how they are designed to blend the macro with the micro. You will grow more and more familiar with not only applying these strategies to your instruction, but also with the process of strategic blended learning instruction in general. Soon enough, you will become comfortable vetting and tweaking existing strategies as needed and, eventually, designing your own blended learning instructional plans. You are closer than you might think. You are ready to become a blended learning master.

Go forth with boldness.

**The Bold School Framework
for Strategic Blended Learning™**

A GUIDE	
Step 1	**Identify Desired Academic Outcome(s)** 1. What skill or skills do I want to cultivate in students? 2. What priority standards will be addressed in this lesson?
Step 2	**Select a Goal-Aligned Instructional Strategy That *Works*** 1. What high effect size instructional strategy or strategies will I leverage to meet the academic outcomes in Step 1? 2. What will my students be doing in this lesson? (e.g., Concept Mapping .64) 3. What will I be doing in this lesson? (e.g., Direct Instruction .60)
Step 3	**Choose Digital Tool** 1. What digital tool or tools can I use to elevate the chosen high effect size strategy? 2. How will these tools make me more efficient and effective? 3. How will the tools elevate or increase the rigor or relevance of student learning? 4. Will these tools allow me to double down on instructional strategies where I am my most skillful, or will they be a distraction to me or my students?
Step 4	**Plan Blended Instruction** 1. How will I plan this lesson strategically with rigorous and relevant academic outcomes in mind? 2. What will I be doing, and what will the students be doing throughout the class?

A GUIDE	
Step 5	**Self-Assess Your Plans and Progress with a Framework**
	Rigor/Relevance Framework:
	1. Are learning tasks moving students out of Quad A (low rigor/low relevance) and toward Quad D (high rigor/high relevance)?
	2. *Rigor:* Do questions or learning tasks require that students use the higher levels of cognition in Bloom's Knowledge Taxonomy? Are students evaluating, synthesizing, analyzing, and/or creating content?
	3. *Relevance:* Will students be able to apply newly acquired knowledge across disciplines and/or to real-world predictable or unpredictable situations? Will students grasp that their learning is relevant to circumstances beyond the class content at hand?

PART 2: a GUIDE to BOLD, BLENDED instructional STRATEGIES

Eleven chapters follow, each dedicated to a specific blended learning instructional strategy. Some things to keep in mind as you read these chapters:

Start on page one. Bold school means being goal oriented and strategic. It means being deliberate and purposeful. This requires context (and courage) so that you can make decisions within the larger understanding of a situation rather than making them in the dark. Without context, you won't know if you are moving toward your goals. The context that comes before these pages is integral to understanding the content that comes after these pages.

Each chapter follows the same structure. Drawing from my coaching experience, I start with a story about someone I've worked with to triple down on what that teacher does best and turn her into a blended learning master. (Note that names and certain identifying details have been changed.) In each chapter, I point out what was missing in a teacher's instruction and the things the teacher needed to learn to make a few simple shifts for big gains.

Then I use the Bold School Framework for Strategic Blended Learning to reimagine the instructional plan so that it's designed to meet intended academic outcomes through instructional strategies that *work* and with digital tools that elevate instruction. Each plan is then vetted against the Rigor/Relevance Framework®.

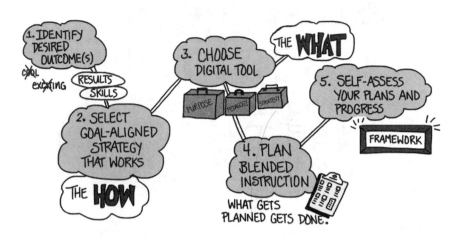

I suggest reading all of the strategies chapters. Not only might you be surprised by how applicable they all are to any discipline and grade, you will also find takeaways in each that can improve your blended instructional plans in general.

All academic outcomes are drawn from real, priority standards. If this is going to be helpful to you, it must be relevant to your real world. I know that your livelihood depends on meeting standards and expectations, and I will not waste your time with fantasy. I'm not going to show you something because it's cool or of the moment. I'm going to show you something because it allows you to achieve what you're accountable to. And I will show you strategies and tools that help you meet standards more efficiently and effectively.

In the Bold School Framework, note that two additions are made to be of service, but are not technical parts of the framework.

1. At the top of each example, I list the grade level and topic to put the example in context.
2. In Step 3, *Choose the Digital Tool*, I list additional digital tool options that would also advance the strategy at hand.

Use the tools you are most comfortable with, especially as you start out. You might also have tools in mind that I don't list. So long as you feel comfortable using a digital tool strategically and it won't distract your students from learning goals, use it.

Keep in mind that new technologies are introduced all the time. At some point, the tools in these pages might no longer be the most useful for advancing the strategy. New tools that are even stronger could come along. The point is to help you practice strategies with this book serving as a detailed guide. But with time, the ultimate point of this book is to set you free by making you so comfortable with the blended instructional strategies in its pages that you feel ready to design your own blended instruction. Soon enough, you will find yourself capable of researching, vetting, and selecting digital tools on your own. My technology recommendations in each chapter are just that: recommendations.

In the examples of these strategies implemented, I tried to include a range of subject areas and grade levels. Please know, though, that these strategies can be adapted for any subject area or grade level. I realize it can sometimes be challenging to adapt a strategy to your needs when you've seen it explained in terms that don't apply to you. But we're bold school. And we care about students first. Don't let this be a reason to disregard a strategy. Instead, find someone you work with to help you think through the process of adapting a strategy that you know will serve you and your students well. In turn, you'll help spread the bold school attitude.

───────

You are now ready to dive in, except for one last thing: an effect-size-driven pep talk for your students—and you.

One of the most impressive instructional strategies out there centers on cultivating high self-expectations. With a 1.33 effect size (Hattie, 2015), we are talking massive growth potential when implemented with fidelity. One of the most inspiring examples about the power of expectations is the true story of Coach Ken

Carter, depicted in the 2005 film "Coach Carter." Ken Carter (played by Samuel L. Jackson) took a job as the basketball coach at a failing inner city school in California with seven straight years of an AYP score of one. (What follows is a massive spoiler alert of the movie version of this incredible story, but for a cause!)

As a member of the faculty, Coach Carter understood that he too was responsible for the futures of his students. For the students of Richmond High School, history said that many of their futures would not include high school graduation or college. Many would likely include crime and prison.

Coach Carter refused to lower expectations of his players. Instead, he made each sign a contract committing to attend all classes and sit in the front row, wear a tie on game day, refer to everyone as sir and ma'am, and get a 2.3 GPA—0.3 points higher than the school's requirement for students to play sports. Failure to meet the contract would mean no more basketball.

To many faculty members at Richmond, Coach Carter's elevated expectations felt foreign, even aggravating. Coach Carter asked that teachers file progress reports of his players, and some resisted because it meant more work. Once they finally delivered, Coach Carter learned that too many on his team were still failing and not showing up for class. Even though his players were fresh off a tournament win and riding high, the next day, Coach Carter put a giant padlock on the gym door with a sign that read, "Practice cancelled, report to the library."

Coach Carter refused to resume basketball practice until every single member of the team had a 2.3 GPA or higher. Practice became study hall, while games were forfeited. Students, faculty, and, parents alike erupted in protest. To some, they missed their beloved basketball. To others, they felt that Coach Carter had taken away the only hope for these boys.

Yet Coach Carter remained undeterred. He did not buckle to pressure coming in from all sides to call off the lockout. He believed that these kids' futures were far more important than a sport and that their high expectations of themselves as students were far more important than the noise coming from the community. Coach Carter was playing the long game on behalf of his students, and he was playing against many on campus who were acting like the opposing team.

The board convened to hold a vote on ending the lockout. Coach Carter declared that if the board voted to resume basketball, they would be sending a message to students that athletes are above the rules and that sports are more important than academics. He refused to be part of such a message. So when the board voted in favor of reversing the lockout, he resigned. He went to his office to gather his belongings and leave.

Upon entering the gym, Coach Carter found all of his players sitting at desks on the basketball court. The board can end the lockout, they said, but they can't make us play. So convinced had his team become that academics were the key to hopeful futures that they, too, had grown unwilling to abandon their learning. Coach Carter's relentless persistence to hold these students to high expectations wore off on the students themselves. Shortly after, they met their team goal: each player got at least a 2.3 GPA. Basketball was back on.

The team went on to play in the high school playoffs and lose to the top ranked St. Francis by just two points in the very last few seconds.

After the game, Coach Carter says to his crestfallen players, "You men played like champions. You never gave up. And champions hold their heads high. What you achieved goes way beyond the win-loss column . . . You've achieved something some people spend their whole lives trying to find. What you achieved is that ever-elusive victory within. And gentleman, I am so proud of you."

The team didn't win the state championship. But they won something so much better, so much more lasting. They won high expectations for themselves. Five of the players won college scholarships, and six went onto college. By all accounts, this team beat the odds, thanks to someone *finally* believing in them and pushing them to believe in themselves.

As you read each instructional strategy, please put an instructional strategy of holding your students—every last one of them—to high expectations in front of it. Let high expectations

STUDENT ACHIEVEMENT

BLENDED LEARNING MOVES THE NEEDLE OF LEARNER *achievement*

permeate everything you do in the classroom. After all, it's a strategy that *works* in moving the needle of achievement. That's what we bold schoolers care about most.

Tell your students every day that you believe in them and you know they can learn and grow. Point out moments and evidence of progress to each. See the talents of all your students, and celebrate them with each kid and the class. Celebrate successes. Celebrate failures— and reframe as opportunities to learn, overcome challenges, and discover perseverance and resilience. Make high expectations part of your students' everyday at school.

And make it part of your everyday, too. By reading this book, you already are. You are reading closely, thinking, absorbing, changing your mindset to bold school. You showed up and you care. That's all I need to know to have high expectations for you as you set out to achieve big blended instruction goals. I expect you to become one helluva blended learning teacher. Let me know how it goes so I can celebrate your successes with you.

CHAPTER 3
BLENDED LEARNING
instructional strategy:
INTERACTIVE VIDEO METHOD

The scene opens on a seventh-grade teacher in her early 40s named Allison. She's got straight, dark brown hair that hits just below her shoulders. She's of about average height. She's in black pants and a comfortable blue sweater. And comfortable shoes to boot, as she will spend most of the day on her feet.

But for as many times as I've seen the scene that follows, she could be most any teacher attempting a first blended learning class or to use a technology for the first time. She could be you. Perhaps this scene will feel as familiar to you as it does to me as a coach who's worked with hundreds of educators on mastering blended learning. In this case, I was beginning my coaching work with Allison by observing her approach to blended learning.

Allison had developed an affinity for EdPuzzle, which allowed her to create interactive video as the centerpiece of her lesson. EdPuzzle is a really cool technology. Like a moth to a flame, she was drawn to its appeal to students and its ability to, in short, replicate her skillset to the effect of another teacher helping her guide more students at once. In preparation for this lesson she uploaded to EdPuzzle a Khan Academy video about adding and subtracting negative numbers. (She could have also imported one from YouTube or most anywhere or made one on her phone.) She then embedded the video with questions and prompts to guide students through the process of watching the video and thinking about content. As a student moves through the video, EdPuzzle automatically stops at each embedded question or prompt, and it will not resume the video until a student has responded.

However, Allison had decided also to bring not one, not two, but three additional technologies into the lesson. The lesson uses a station rotation model, so students would rotate from one station to the next. This was meant to be about blended learning, after all, so Allison thought that each station had to make use of technology. The first station used the EdPuzzle video. At the next station, students used Google Forms and TodaysMeet—both of which were new to the kids—to solve a math problem collaboratively. And at the third station, Allison planned to guide students through a problem solving exercise, after which they would submit responses and explanations using SurveyMonkey. I know you're thinking what I was thinking—wow, that's a lot.

As I sat in the classroom ready to observe her first attempt at an interactive video blended learning class, Allison stood at the front, putting some last minute touches on the plan as her students streamed in. Once all the kids arrived, she spent a few minutes doing direct instruction about negative numbers to impart some foundational knowledge. Then she put the kids in groups, assigned each to a station, and let the games begin.

One problem: the video Allison chose was 12 minutes long. With the embedded questions, it was taking the kids at the EdPuzzle video station way longer to get through the video than the 15 minutes she had allotted for each rotation. That station was a bottleneck slowing all the other stations down. It's a common mistake for first-time station rotation and interactive video users.

Allison's plan was to spend most of her time at the third station guiding students through a math question. But she kept getting pulled away. The kids at the second station were struggling to master Google Forms and TodaysMeet, while the kids at station one needed help with URLs and student login information. In fits and starts, the kids at station three were left to attempt the problem on their own, at times wandering off task.

Time passed and over at station one, the EdPuzzle students were still wading through the cumbersome video, and by now, all the other students were getting restless and impatient at their

"WELL, I'M NEVER DOING THAT AGAIN."

stations. Finally, the video group was done, so all students rotated. And the mayhem started again. Allison was unable to focus on her students at station three because, again, the kids at stations one and two working with new technologies needed her help. Allison paid a quick visit to the students using EdPuzzle to find them once again moving slowly through the long video, as her kids at station three continued to wait for her to return.

The scene unfolded with increasing chaos until, mercifully, the bell rang. As her students gathered their belongings and exited the classroom, Allison collapsed in her chair and said to me, "Well, I'm never doing that again."

I want to start the instructional strategies part of this book with Allison's lesson not just because, when used strategically, interactive video has an impressive .54 effect size (Hattie, 2015); I want to start with Allison also because I have seen great teachers new to blended learning or a technology give up again and again. The class at best feels clunky, or at worst spirals out of the teacher's control. The teacher doesn't know how to manage all the moving parts. The kids begin to get restless. And mercy only comes with the sound of the bell. The teacher declares blended learning or technology is not for her.

Except not us. Not anymore. We're bold school. And as bold schoolers, we have grit and we learn and we persevere. We persevere because our students depend on us to prepare them for their futures, not ours. And today, this requires that we create an environment for our students where they can both acquire and apply new skills while leveraging innovative technologies to do so. It requires strategic blended learning.

In Chapter 2, we talked about how strategic plans

★ INTERACTIVE VIDEO .54 EFFECT SIZE!

STRATEGY

NAIL IT!

allow you to retrace steps backward and forward so that you can see why you succeeded or failed. You might be thinking, "If I've never been strategic in my attempts at blended instruction, how do I even begin if I can't understand why I've failed in the past? Won't I still be working from a foundation without insights and that I don't understand?" Yep, you will—unless you do like Simba and boldly declare that you will not let your past define your future.

Yes, that was a "Lion King" reference, and I'm not ashamed. We can all pretend we're too old and mature for that movie, or we can just admit what we know to be true: that we're never too old to look back to an animated classic chock full of superfluous musical numbers.

To refresh, Mufasa—lion king of the Pride Lands of Africa— falls off a cliff to his death when he attempts to save his son, Simba, a young cub, from a herd of wildebeest. The entire stamp -ede was surreptitiously orchestrated by Mufasa's jealous younger brother, Scar, in an attempt to kill Simba and take his place as first in line to the throne (sniff).

Racked with guilt over his father's death, Simba flees the kingdom and tries to get all "hakuna matata" as he runs from his past. Years later, though, his past catches up to him, when he chances into his childhood best friend, Nala. Nala tells him that he must return to the kingdom because it has fallen into decay and drought under Scar's cruel reign. Simba is unwilling to face his past, so he runs off again. He eventually crosses paths with the baboon shaman Rafiki, who reminds Simba of the circle of life and that his dad would have wanted him to take his rightful place as king.

"Oh yes, the past can hurt," Rafiki says to Simba. "But you can either run from it or learn from it."

Ah, what is a Disney movie if not the guarantee of a life lesson and a good cry.

The moral of the story? Oh yes, the blended learning mistakes of your past can hurt. But you can either run from them or learn from them.

Bold schoolers do not run. We learn.

Where should you begin if your past attempts at blended learning have been haphazard and without strategy? Right here. You begin by not running. You begin by remembering that mistakes are feedback. And then you get guidance from this book, or any resource that will teach you how to become strategic. (But you're here, so you might as well stick around!) Once you are in that strategic mindset, I assure you, you will still make mistakes. But you will be able to point to why. Then you will not repeat that mistake again. And with just a little time and effort, you will make fewer and fewer mistakes. Even still, when you do err off course, from this bold school place, there's nothing to run from. There are only new experiences that provide new data points. There's no such thing as failure, just feedback.

Speaking of, let's look at the feedback Allison's experience revealed. As I watched her slip into frenzy in her classroom, what was off track was evident and easily fixable. More often than not, I observe teachers who have strong foundational teaching skills and are excellent with certain instructional strategies. More often than not, when blended instruction throws these otherwise fantastic teachers off their game, they are just few technicalities and one strategic plan away from nailing it. This was the case with Allison. She only needed to learn a couple of technical things to improve the integration of interactive video into effective instruction, and then she would be ready to design a strategic and awesome lesson that leveraged interactive video.

Trust me when I say, this is almost always the case with blended learning: we just need a few simple shifts with big gains. In other words, we just need to look back briefly, learn from our past mistakes, and then move forward with new knowledge, ready to tackle any challenge. Like Simba, who boldly became King of the Pride Lands of Africa. I will stop short of saying you, too, can boldly become King or Queen of the Pride Lands of Blended Learning. I won't say it. Because that would be cheesy. But you can! Go ahead . . . I won't tell anyone.

Here's what Allison needed to learn:

1. *Start with the academic outcome.* You know this by now, but Allison had yet to learn this point. Instead of beginning the process of planning her blended learning class first with the desired academic outcomes, she started with the bright shiny object. As a result, her use of EdPuzzle (and all of the other tech tools, for that matter) was not strategic nor designed with the end goal in mind.

EdPuzzle is an incredible tool, and its appeal is strong. It can, in effect, multiply the number of teachers in the room. The video tool means both you and Sal Kahn can be teaching the same content to the same students at the same time. Hell, if you make a video yourself, then you've accomplished the once impossible dream every teacher has had at some point—to clone him or herself!

What Allison didn't yet understand was that no matter how awesome a technology can be, its ability to advance student learning depends entirely on the human being who decides to use it. Technologies are by no means magic bullets. But when used strategically, they can help teachers be so much more efficient and effective in their roles and allow students to learn and obtain skills in ways that are exciting and pertinent to 21st century competencies.

2. *Avoid technology for technology's sake.* We know this now. (And Allison does, too.) To make for a successful blended learning class, strategic EdPuzzle use was all she needed, especially this early in her journey. Allison made a common mistake of those new to blended learning: piling on as many tech tools as possible because this was, after all, blended learning. Yes, but the main goal is still learning academic concepts and developing new skills. Because Allison introduced so many new tech tools at once, on top of a new math concept, the kids were distracted by having to learn new technologies. And Allison was distracted by having to teach those technologies. Everyone's eye was taken off the academic ball: learning math skills.

Since EdPuzzle was the most important tech tool to the lesson and since it was new to everyone involved, it was all she needed. At station two, the kids would have been able to focus on the math concept had they been left to use old school pen and paper. (Pen and paper? Really? Yes, I said pen and paper . . . in a book about blended learning.) There are cases where sometimes kids are better off with old school tools. And there are cases where more than one technology tool can enhance instruction and learning in the classroom. But we must build up to this. Introduce technology tools only once you have first been able to learn them and after you've been able to teach your students how to use them—in a manner and at a time where it does not take away, but adds to, learning an academic concept.

Pace yourself. This is ultimately still about academic concepts and lifelong skills.

3. *Size matters:* The 12-minute video was way too long. In 2015, the average length watched of a single online video was about 2 minutes and 42 seconds (Statistic Brain, 2016). And keep in mind that embedded questions stretch out the exercise that much longer. Use videos in the two-to-four minute range.

4. *Question with purpose.* After reviewing Allison's questions, all of them were at level one on Bloom's Knowledge Taxonomy and none pertained to anything relevant outside of the classroom. Educators often ask me how many questions they should ask in embedded video. I typically tell them to try to get at least one from each level of Bloom's. This way you ensure that you are pushing kids to think rigorously. I also remind them that without rigorous questions, the strategy reduces to computer-assisted instruction, which has an effect size of only .45 (Hattie, 2015).

The question of relevance remains. I usually suggest to teachers that they use the interactive video method in a station rotation model. Sometimes the video itself is real-world relevant. But when it's not, it can be challenging (but not impossible) to succinctly bring relevance into an interactive video. The station rotation model creates other opportunities for relevance. This is important because when we connect an academic concept to the world beyond school, students understand that what they are learning matters and is pertinent to life beyond school and the future.

In the case of Allison's class, she could have used the concept of a budget to bridge negative numbers to the outside world. She could ask students to identify where there is a negative number using an example of a student who forgets today's lunch money. The student starts the day with zero dollars and then has to borrow $5 from a friend to buy lunch. In addition to asking students to identify where in that real-life scenario there is a negative number, additional calculations could be asked of the students, e.g., from the position of owing $5, how much money does the student need to have $10. With that simple move, some basic relevance has been achieved.

5. *There are two methodologies for strategic interactive video use:*

   a. *Show & Tell:* Show a video to students and let them tell you their reflections/responses to questions in writing or via multimedia throughout the video or at the video's conclusion.

   b. *Tell & Show:* The viewer initially tells the teacher (via embedded prompts or questions at the start of the video) what he thinks the answer is to a question, his opinion regarding an issue, and/or his thoughts based on a prompt. The viewer is then shown a video so that he can make determinations as to whether or not his original assertions were accurate, justified, etc. Example: "Where in this worked math problem does the student make a mistake? What does the student need to do to correct it?" Show students in the conclusion of the video whether or not their assertions were accurate and/or matched with predetermined proficiency.

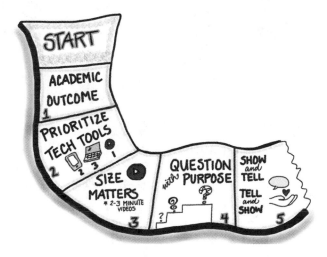

By following one of these two methods, you will avoid just peppering in lots of questions without a clear purpose. Instead, questions will help move students toward a specific learning goal.

———

Building on what we've gleaned from Allison's experience, let's plan a strategic interactive video lesson using the Bold School Framework.

The Bold School Framework
for Strategic Blended Learning™

INTERACTIVE VIDEO	
Topic: Middle School—Science, Weather and Climate	
Step 1	**Identify Desired Academic Outcome(s)** 1. Ask and answer questions. 2. Define problems. 3. Compare concepts.
Step 2	**Select a Goal-Aligned Instructional Strategy That *Works*** *Interactive Video Method* (.54 effect size) (Hattie, 2015) To enhance the effectiveness of this strategy, it should come after teacher-delivered core instruction and be used within a station rotation model. Through the application of teacher-embedded rigorous questions or prompts in a video, interactive video allows students to reinforce learning and deepen cognition around core ideas.
Step 3	**Choose Digital Tool(s)** *EdPuzzle* EdPuzzle allows the teacher to replicate her skillset and reach more students through direct instruction at one time. While students are gathering information and answering questions via interactive video, the teacher can spend time coaching students through a different learning task. *Other strategic digital tool options:* Screencast-o-matic, Vialogues
Step 4	**Plan Blended Instruction** The teacher begins by exposing students to core ideas before sending them to different stations to supplement and support new learning. Students stay at each station for 12–15 minutes.

INTERACTIVE VIDEO	
Topic: **Middle School—Science, Weather and Climate**	
Step 4 (cont.)	*Station 1: Interactive video.* The teacher creates a brief three-minute video lecture on the fundamental differences between climate and weather. Using Show & Tell or Tell & Show, questions that include verbiage from across each level of Bloom's Knowledge Taxonomy and are embedded to increase rigor.
	Station 2: Teacher-led instruction. For increased relevance, the teacher guides students through an exercise that involves determining where in the United States different weather events are or are not likely based on various climates across the country.
	Station 3: Collaborative activities station. Students work together to consider how various circumstances change in different climates and/or seasons.
Step 5	**Self-Assess Your Plans and Progress with a Framework**
	Rigor/Relevance Framework: Are learning tasks moving students out of Quad A (low rigor/low relevance) and toward Quad D (high rigor/high relevance)?
	Rigor: As questions move up Bloom's Knowledge Taxonomy, they naturally elicit more complex thinking. Ensure that at least some embedded video questions ask students to evaluate different pieces of information, ideally that first depend on analysis and synthesis and build comparative and judgment skills. For example, compare the elements that define climate to those that define weather. Based on the climate in the Southwest of the United States, what judgments can you make about its weather during the summer and winter? Based on the winter weather of the Northeast, what judgments can you make about its climate?

INTERACTIVE VIDEO	
Topic: Middle School—Science, Weather and Climate	
Step 5 **(cont.)**	*Relevance:* Ways to bring relevance to this lesson could include drawing the academic concept to another discipline or to a real-world situation these seventh graders could imagine. In this class design, relevance could be addressed in Stations 2 and 3. Students could be asked to consider if Hurricane Katrina was a weather or a climate event and where in the United States such hurricanes are and are not likely to happen and why. They could be asked to outline the implications of a family that moved from Phoenix, Arizona (warm climate) to Rochester, Minnesota (cold climate). Examples could be: more money spent on heating, less on air conditioning; snow tires would be needed for cars; the family would need to buy a winter wardrobe, etc. Students could be asked to write and record a weather forecast on behalf of a (fictional) local television weatherman in Boston for a day in January.

The Station Rotation Model

The station rotation model can be a great way for students to interact with an academic concept through a range of mediums and through both rigorous and relevant examples. I'm a big fan of using this class design with interactive video because the power of video is that it's like having more than one teacher in the room. This allows the teacher to spend more time guiding students at a station or delivering remediation.

The ideal rotation design has three stations:

1. *Interactive video:* A group of students engages with a 2–4 minute video with questions embedded by the teacher.

2. *Teacher-led instruction:* The teacher guides a group of students through a question or problem.

3. *Collaborative activities and stations:* A group of students work together to solve a problem or answer a question. Unless teacher and students are already familiar with a collaborative technology, students should use paper and pencil to submit work.

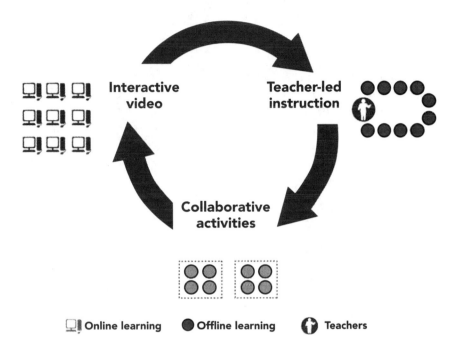

Interactive video

Teacher-led instruction

Collaborative activities

🖥️ Online learning   ⬤ Offline learning   ⬤ Teachers

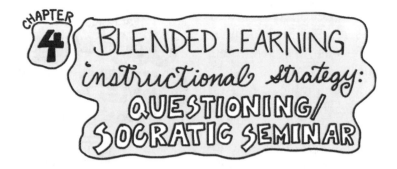

CHAPTER 4

BLENDED LEARNING
instructional strategy:
QUESTIONING/
SOCRATIC SEMINAR

"Bueller? . . . Bueller? . . . Bueller?"

One word, on loop, in total monotone, and we have a cinematic teaching icon.

How could we ever repay John Hughes for so perfectly capturing the awkwardness, joys, pains, and fun of the suburban high school experience in his gems like "Sixteen Candles," "The Breakfast Club," "Pretty in Pink," to name just a few?

For John Hughes fans who went on to become teachers, the favorite, though, is often the inimitable "Ferris Bueller's Day Off." What high school student at the time didn't leave that movie with the fantasy of ditching school to tear around in a 1961 Ferrari 250 GT California and end up lip-syncing Wayne Newton's cover of "Danke Schoen" in a German-American heritage parade? And what teacher since hasn't pointed to the economics teacher played by Ben Stein as what *not* to do in the classroom? In Stein's brief, but brilliant performance, he nails the art of boring the crap out of students with listless lecturing and rapid-fire, dull questions.

As Stein's character drones on about the Smoot-Hawley Tariff Act, he repeatedly interrupts himself to ask the students a string of nothing more than fill-in-the-blank questions. The camera closes in tight on bored student after bored student. One blows bright pink bubbles with her gum. Another is asleep, with the desk drool to prove it. Several stare blankly forward, mouths

agape in silence, as not one answers any of Stein's questions. He is left to answer them all himself.

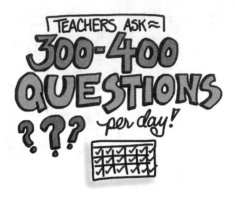

It's a memorable scene. And one any teacher lives in fear of replicating in real life.

Fortunately, I rarely encounter teachers who speak in a flatness even nearing that of Ben Stein. But unfortunately, I do often encounter teachers who fire off a stream of low rigor questions at students. Teachers ask between 300–400 questions every day and even as many as 120 per hour (Vogler, 2008). In most cases, these are quantity-over-quality questions that do not drive learning, à la Ben Stein's character. With this many questions, it's just not possible that they can be rigorous in nature and leave students enough time to reflect and answer thoughtfully. No danke schoen!

Questions will always be part of instruction and learning. Because they should be! They are a natural part of thinking and conversing in school, life, and careers. As an instructional strategy, questioning has an effect size of .48 (Hattie, 2015). This is not off the charts, but it is downright solid; questioning, when integrated strategically into activities like Socratic seminars, gets you more than a year's worth of growth in a year's worth of time when used with fidelity. When questions are intentionally tied to academic goals, they can drive motivation, capture students' attention, hone thinking skills, help students synthesize and evaluate information, push them to bank more knowledge, and also encourage their curiosity (Vogler, 2008).

Relative to the ease with which this instructional strategy can be used (ahem, so long as it's used *strategically*), questioning is a great tool for any teacher to have in his or her back pocket. It's also a space where new technologies have opened the door for teachers to ensure that every last student in the classroom—not just those who volunteer or who are called upon to answer questions—is involved, engaged, and learning.

There are also scores of teachers out there who love and can be really great at questioning. Take Pablo, a teacher I worked with as a coach. This man was easily Socrates' number one fan, and Socratic seminars were a common occurrence in his classroom. The Socratic Method, from which Socratic seminars are derived, is about asking questions in search of a truth. It's about asking questions whose value resides in their exploration, not their answer. Socrates would ask his students question after question until a contradiction was exposed, thus laying bare a fallacy in the initial thinking and leading to the discovery of a new truth. When questions push toward a new discovery or truth, they naturally require that a person think with increasing complexity and depth. When tied to an academic outcome and applied with strategy, the Socratic Method and Socratic seminars can be an effective way to ask questions and help kids reach a new level of understanding.

As someone who valued the power of the Socratic Method, Pablo's intentions were pure and passionate, yet his execution was incomplete. The thing was, you wouldn't necessarily have known it by observing him in action; his seminars were engaging and most of his students were actively participating. What was missing were rigorous questions. Almost all of the questions he asked were in the lower levels of Bloom's Taxonomy, keeping his students stuck in Quad A thinking.

Pablo loved the Socratic seminar, as did his kids. In terms of passion, interest, and engagement, I wasn't about to take that away from him or his students. What good would it have done to tell Pablo to stop doing what he loved and instead try something he didn't enjoy? Nope, that ain't bold school. That would have pushed Pablo, and all his experience and wisdom, out of the blended learning equation. Instead, we doubled down—no, tripled down—on Pablo's natural talents and layered it with strategic planning and technology use. With just a few simple shifts, Pablo did become a bold school, blended learning master of his beloved Socratic seminar.

What Pablo needed to learn:

1. *What gets scripted gets asked.* On the flip, what doesn't get scripted risks making a Ben Stein of you. When questions are not pre-planned, they're devised on the fly, which all but guarantees they will be low rigor. It's no easy task to come up with high-rigor questions when they're off the cuff. Spontaneous questions are almost always nothing more than recall in nature. They devolve into a back and forth of teachers firing off simple questions and students firing back simple answers.

The goal of questions is not to get kids to answer; it's to get them to *think.* Thinking questions are rigorous questions. And rigorous questions require thinking of teachers. Take time before a Socratic seminar to come up with thoughtful, increasingly complex questions and write them down to serve as a script for your instruction.

2. *Make sure questions address multiple levels of cognition.* When designing questions refer to each level of Bloom's Taxonomy, the vertical and rigor axis of the Rigor/Relevance Framework:

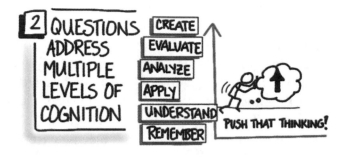

Make it a goal to use questions to guide your students through increasingly complex levels of cognition, scaffolding as needed. Cross-reference the verbiage from the taxonomy to check that questions get to high levels of rigor. (See Appendix E for Verb List by Quadrant and Appendix G for Teacher Question Stems by Quadrant.) Do not let any Socratic seminar unfold without at least one question from every level of the taxonomy. If questions do not get kids analyzing, synthesizing, and evaluating, new understanding will likely not be achieved. If they do, when paired with relevance, your students are moving closer and closer to Quad D learning. (Tip: Go to leadered.com/resources/white-papers.php to check out Dr. Bill Daggett's white paper *Rigor/ Relevance Framework®: A Guide to Focusing Resources to Increase Student Performance.*)

3. *Put scripted questions into technologies beforehand.* There is one risk of questioning that no teacher, however masterful, can ever humanly, totally avoid. Yet tech-nologies can. Questioning without the boost of purposeful technology integration holds the caveat that the teacher will not reach every student. This is just human nature. The shyer or more introverted kids are going to be less likely to raise their hands to answer questions. Sometimes these kids just never talk in class. Can you blame them? Let's face it,

sticking your young hand in the air and subjecting yourself to the judgment of both your teacher and peers can be a pretty risky proposition. Until technologies, one of the old work-arounds was cold calling these kids. Yet this is known as a highly ineffective option (Stanford Teaching Commons, n.d.). Introverted learners require reflection and time, if even just a few seconds, to think before answering (Helgoe, 2010). To these students, cold calling is their worst nightmare. What's more, if teachers are known to cold call, many students, introverted or otherwise, will spend the lion's share of their thinking energy in that class praying they do not get cold called for fear of embarrassing themselves with a rushed answer. And when that unlucky kid does get cold called, the rest of the students often give into their relief and stop thinking entirely.

Enter some awesome technologies like Kahoot!, Nearpod, Poll Everywhere, Twitter, TodaysMeet, and Socrative (to name a few). These tools let all students answer your questions in real time and digitally. Gone are the days where it's just the same handful of students dominating every class. Gone are the days where those quiet students go left behind. Here are the days where technologies are empowering every student in your class to have a voice.

By leveraging technology tools in questioning, all students get the opportunity to answer your pre-planned, rigorous questions. All students get the opportunity to think on multiple levels, come to new understanding, and reach learning goals. This is blended learning at its best.

Added bonus? By pre-planning your questions and using technologies to reach all students, you will not be nearly as tired after a questioning class. Just ask Pablo, who now is a blended learning Socratic master. The process of trying to come up with questions *as* he was lecturing would leave him drained. When I first told him that pre-planning questions and inputting them into tech tools would elevate his teaching to new levels, his response was, "That sounds like a total pain." But he agreed to give it a go. All it took was one bold school blended learning Socratic seminar for him to be convinced that front-loading the strategic planning left him invigorated by a truly engaging, challenging, and fun session with and for his students. Another bonus: those questions are already locked and loaded for next year's crop of students. Only slight modifications will be needed to differentiate according to that group's needs.

Building from Pablo's class, let's plan a strategic questioning lesson using the Bold School Framework.

**The Bold School Framework
for Strategic Blended Learning™**

QUESTIONING/SOCRATIC SEMINAR *Topic:* High School—ELA, Reading and Analyzing Poetry	
Step 1	**Identify Desired Academic Outcome(s)** 1. Read to determine what text says explicitly. 2. Read to make logical inferences. 3. Cite text evidence when writing.
Step 2	**Select a Goal-Aligned Instructional Strategy That *Works*** *Questioning/Socratic Seminar* (.48 effect size) (Hattie, 2015) This strategy relies on a series of questions to guide students' thinking toward high levels of rigor and complexity. The effectiveness of questioning depends on the rigor of questions used, making teacher pre-planning and assessment of questions critical. When questions are of high rigor and directly related to learning materials and desired academic outcomes, student thinking is challenged and new understanding is more likely to be achieved.
Step 3	**Choose Digital Tool(s)** *Nearpod* The teacher will leverage Nearpod as a digital medium through which he can give students access to the poem and his pre-planned and rigorous questions or prompts for Socratic seminar. The tool lets students follow the teacher as he provides direct instruction, so fewer get lost or off track. As Nearpod allows everyone in the class to see all students' answers, meaningful discussion is enhanced, as it is now based not only on the questions, but also everyone's answers. *Other strategic digital tool options:* Google Forms, Kahoot!, Plickers, Poll Everywhere, Socrative, Twitter

QUESTIONING/SOCRATIC SEMINAR	
Topic: **High School—ELA, Reading and Analyzing Poetry**	
Step 4	**Plan Blended Instruction** The students will read "Hope is the Thing with Feathers" by Emily Dickinson as discussion material. The teacher will use Bloom's Taxonomy to pre-plan questions that account for and require from students all levels of thinking. In the seminar, students will be asked to provide explanations, justifications, etc., of their interpretations of the poem, both in spoken and written form. The teacher will guide access to questions and determine which need verbal or written prompts. The teacher will use other examples of examining words and inferring meaning to ensure relevance.
Step 5	**Self-Assess Your Plans and Progress with a Framework** *Rigor/Relevance Framework:* Are learning tasks moving students out of Quad A (low rigor/low relevance) and toward Quad D (high rigor/high relevance)? *Rigor:* This lesson's academic outcome demands deeper cognition. If questions remain of low rigor, the academic outcome cannot be achieved. The teacher can cross-reference all questions to ensure that at least some qualify as achieving rigorous levels of cognition. The teacher could ask students to make a judgment about Dickinson's general feelings about hope and guide students to analyze word use, make inferences, and arrive at a determination. Students could be asked to try to determine how their own experiences and feelings about hope changed their perception of the poem.

QUESTIONING/SOCRATIC SEMINAR	
Topic: **High School—ELA, Reading and Analyzing Poetry**	
Step 5 **(cont.)**	*Relevance:* How can the analysis of a poem relate to other disciplines or areas of the real world? (Note: Recall "Dead Poets Society"? Watch John Keating, master of bringing relevance to poems, for inspiration.) To achieve relevance in this seminar, questions could extend to include how other types of writing, not just poetry, require inference and analysis. The point could be made that words, even those outside of poems, almost always hold some ambiguity and require context and inference for understanding. An example that could be The United States Constitution, which has a whole court system built to analyze and evaluate its words to the point of drawing contextual conclusions. Questions could be asked to guide students to understand the significance of the ambiguity of the Constitution's text. An example: Just as you brought your own experience and opinions to the understanding of Dickinson's poem, is it possible that Supreme Court Justices might bring their experiences and opinions to the interpretation of law? And what might the effects of this be? The point is to ensure that at least one cohesive connection to the outside world is made so that students understand that analyzing words is contextual and a skill used in life and careers. Using the relevance continuum, vet questions for relevance and make sure at least one example achieves Quad B. When used in conjunction with Quad C thinking throughout the class, Quad D will be achieved.

CHAPTER 5
BLENDED LEARNING
instructional strategy:
VOCABULARY PROGRAMS

One of the great mysteries of education is why we don't teach kids vocabulary how they learn it. Have you ever been around a small child learning to speak? You obviously have. Great, then you know how kids learn and remember words.

Back when my daughter was still small enough to fit in my arms, I would point to objects and say the word. I would point to our dog and say, "dog." Then I'd turn her toward me, point to myself, and say, "boss." Then I'd turn her around to point to my wife and say, "Daddy's boss." Teaching my daughter words this way was innate, pure reflex. This is because I intuitively understand, just as you do, that there is no comprehension or retention without picturing. And I can prove it in 10 seconds.

Flower. Immense. Chair. Succinctly. Philosophize. Arid. Floccinaucinihilipilification. Green. Beaker. Wait, what? Flocciwhat?

Exactly.

Up to "floccinaucinihilipilification," you were with me, right? And you also probably had images flash to mind for each word. Flower: you might have pictured a red rose. Immense: something huge. Chair: perhaps your desk chair. Succinctly: maybe you imagined a really short sentence. Philosophize: perhaps a black and white image of someone bearded with a pipe came to mind. Arid: a dry desert. And with "floccinaucinihilipilification," I'm sure I lost you. That cognitive reflex to imagine the word as an image shut down. Since the words were a random collection with no unifying relationship, they offered no contextual clues for the meaning of floccinaucinihilipilification. You probably also didn't absorb the words that followed floccinaucinihilipilification because your brain was tripped up by a word it couldn't understand.

Now consider this. Imagine I took an old beaten up car to the auto body shop for an estimate. The mechanic came back to me and said, "Weston, the frame of the car has rust inside and out. The engine took 20 minutes to start. It's missing bolts on the sheet panels. Both axles are torqued, causing the alignment to be off. The torque converter is nearly broken down, so your transmission system is a few trips from being completely shot. At this rate, to get this car into any decent shape, it would cost more than it's worth. I'm afraid to say, this car is a floccinaucinihilipilification. It's just not worth fixing up."

Someone in this situation would probably feel dejected to learn they could get nothing for the old, beaten up car.

Now do you know what "floccinaucinihilipilification" means? You are probably arriving at a pretty accurate guess. Based on the context in which I used the word, you are able to gather that this word has something to do with value and worth, and it likely skews toward the side of having little value or worth.

And you would be correct. Per Dictionary.com, floccinaucinihilipilification is a noun that means, "the estimation of something as valueless." Fun fact, it is "encountered mainly as an example of one of the longest words in the English language." It's also encountered when I coach teachers about how to use blended instruction to teach vocabulary in a way that *works*.

On that point, if I do a Google image search of "old beaten up car" to provide you a visual to associate with floccinaucinihilipilification, your odds of remembering the meaning of this word shoot up that much more.

By now you know what the word floccinaucinihilipilification means, and you are also likely to retain it. (Pronouncing it might be another issue.) This is because it was taught to you using the two most effective ways to learn vocabulary: context and picturing.

Yet for some reason—some very mysterious, perplexing reason—this is not how we teach our students vocabulary. Instead, we give kids a list of words, often random and unrelated to each other, and ask them to find the definition in the dictionary and write it down. Then we hope they'll understand and remember it.

We know that language gap is the main driver of the achievement gap between socioeconomic groups (Hirsch, 2003). A longitudinal study determined that by age three, kids from wealthier families have a working vocabulary of 1,116 words. That number drops to 749 for kids from working-class families and slides all the way down to 525 for kids from families on welfare (Sparks, 2013). Put another way, those kids from higher-class families know 367 words more than those from working-class families. And those kids from welfare families know less than half as many words as their upper-class counterparts. It's no wonder, then, that Hirsch has called growing students' vocabulary the "key to upward mobility" (Sparks, 2013).

Imagine how many floccinaucinihilipilification moments students, especially those from middle and lower-class families, have every day in school. Now multiply that by 10 for our English language learners. Imagine what that means cumulatively for their ability to keep up with new concepts and ideas, year after year. How did you feel when I sandwiched "floccinaucinihilipilification" between arid and green? The confusion you felt, the desperate attempt to search for context clues, and how this impaired your focus on what followed happens to students all the time in school. Your "floccinaucinihilipilification" is kids' "chromosome," "denominator," "analogy." And the only way around these moments of confusion it is to teach vocabulary how kids learn it.

Throughout the 2009–2010 school year, researchers from University of Michigan at Ann Arbor and Michigan State University at East Lansing observed 55 kindergarten teachers from districts of various poverty levels. Rarely did they observe a teacher who delivered structured, formal vocabulary lessons. Instead, most taught vocabulary as it came up, such as when reading a book to students. This created situations where the words these students were taught had little relation to the concepts they were learning at the time, and they usually were not academic words that would advance students' understanding in later grades or other subject areas (Sparks, 2013).

We know this approach doesn't work. Yet most of us are guilty of it. That's OK. Remember Allison (and Simba) in Chapter 3? We're bold school. We don't run from our past mistakes, we learn from them. Decide that this is the moment you will change how you teach vocabulary. And I've got good news for you: a blended learning approach is going to make this so much easier for you and so much more effective for your students.

Brace yourselves: old school doesn't always mean good. Sometimes we get too wrapped up in the tried and true that we forget to question if the tried *is* actually true. Vocabulary instruction is a case where the old and tried way of doing it *is not* true. This is what we as bold schoolers have to keep in mind: when it comes to blended learning, it's not necessarily the old school we want to put back in its rightful place; it's the *wisdom* that we want to lean on, and much of it happens to be old school. But what bold schoolers know is that wisdom can be both old *and* new. Vocabulary instruction is one of these examples where new technologies are creating new wisdom about how to teach students so they will actually comprehend and remember new vocabulary.

Vocabulary is foundational to all learning. Vocabulary understanding directly correlates with reading comprehension. This creates a virtuous cycle effect that can work against or for a child, depending on her vocabulary: the more words a kid knows, the more she can exploit context clues to understand more of what she is reading (Kuhn & Stahl, 1998). And the more she can understand while reading, the more reading she can and likely will do—and learn yet more words.

Simply put, vocabulary is the key to closing the achievement gap. We have no choice; we have to find more effective ways to teach vocabulary. So what do those of us who have remained a little too stuck in the past when it comes to vocabulary instruction need to understand to become bold school blended learning masters of it?

What we all need to learn:

1. *Vocabulary instruction must be formal and structured.* Per John Hattie's research, it's when vocabulary is taught through dedicated instruction that relies on deeper thinking about word meaning that the .62 effect size can be achieved (Hattie, 2015). When vocabulary is taught in an ad hoc, as-it-comes-up manner, it is

usually taught without context or repeat exposure. Kids, then, will be unlikely to comprehend or retain the meaning of the word thrown at them randomly.

2. *Comprehension requires context.* Fans of the American version of "The Office" might recognize this: "The Office" was a mocku-mentary style television show that captured the many absurdities and comical realities of cubicle life in America. The receptionist, Erin (Ellie Kemper), was the type of person who was sweet as can be but just not sharp. She was also earnest in her aim to better herself every day. At one point, this was by way of increasing her vocabulary. In this episode, she says, "My goal was to learn a new word every day, and I must say that it is going immensely."

For me, this is one of those laugh-cry moments. Laugh because it's funny. Cry because it's true. Erin's comment perfectly illustrates the inadequacy of the approach to learning vocabulary that we see all too often in our schools. We ask kids to go to the dictionary, look up a word, write down the defi-nition, and expect they'll understand and remember how to use it without context. Yet scores of studies have made it clear that context is hugely helpful to deriving the meaning of new words and understanding how to use them (Kuhn & Stahl, 1998). And context is integral to achieving the high effect size of vocabulary programs.

3. *There is no comprehension without picturing—and the internet is full of pictures.* There's a boatload of research that shows images and visual cues improve our retention and ability to retrieve information. This makes sense when you consider how the brain works; far more of our sensory cortex, the part of the brain that processes sensory information, is devoted to vision than it is to words (Kouyoumdjian, 2012). The brain is built to remember pic-tures with more accuracy than it is to remember words.

Numerous studies have proven the power of visual imag-ery in learning and retention. In one such study, students were asked to remember various groups of three random words. The students who were asked merely to memorize the words had low recall. The students who were asked to create visualizations of the groups of words recalled the words at a far greater rate (Kouyoumdjian, 2012).

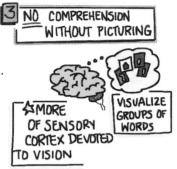

You might have memories of vocabulary lessons where a teacher asked you to cut images from magazines that represented vocabulary. This was a great strategy that worked. The problem was it required teachers to supply a bunch of magazines, and it took way too long for students to flip through them all and find relevant images. So, in most cases, vocabulary instruction defaults to the less cumbersome process of asking students to look up words in a dictionary and memorize meaning.

But today, we can find any image with the one swift internet search. Leveraging simple technologies, we can make use of high effect size vocabulary programs that create rigorous thinking around words—while also promoting retention. This bold school plan is so easy to implement, it's a no brainer.

———————

Building from almost every classroom vocabulary moment ever, let's plan a strategic vocabulary lesson using the Bold School Framework.

The Bold School Framework
for Strategic Blended Learning™

VOCABULARY PROGRAMS	
Topic: High School—Mathematics, Statistics and Probability	
Step 1	**Identify Desired Academic Outcome(s)** 1. Develop understanding of statistical variability. 2. Summarize and describe distributions.
Step 2	**Select a Goal-Aligned Instructional Strategy That *Works*** *Vocabulary Programs* (.62 effect size) (Hattie, 2015) This strategy depends on vocabulary instruction taught in a formal, structured way, where words are related to core concepts being learned and are delivered in context. Students must be exposed to each word at least twice to support comprehension. Picturing will also be added to promote retention.
Step 3	**Choose Digital Tool(s)** *Google image search and Google Docs* Google image search allows students to find a visual representation of each vocabulary word. Using a Google Doc with a teacher-customized and embedded Frayer Model, students will be able to put each vocabulary word in context and enhance rigorous and relevant thinking. *Other strategic digital tool options:* Google Cardboard, Google Slides, Padlet, Popplet

VOCABULARY PROGRAMS	
Topic: High School—Mathematics, Statistics and Probability	
Step 4	**Plan Blended Instruction**
	Before students can solve problems associated with statistics and variability, they need a foundational understanding of keywords and phrases that are associated with each.
	The vocabulary to be learned will be: Median, Mean, Mode, and Range.
	For each word, students will utilize Google image search to find visual representations of each concept. Students will put information about each vocabulary word into a collaborative Google Doc featuring a Frayer Model graphic organizer—with a twist for increased rigor and relevance. The typical Frayer Model includes the word at the center, surrounded by the definition (including the part of speech); a picture or pictures of the example retrieved from a Google image search; characteristics/facts; and non-examples. For Quad D learning, the teacher will customize the Frayer model to include an "application" section so that students consider other circumstances in which the word can be used for relevance.
	Within the Frayer Model, students will include: Visual Example; Definition and Part of Speech; Characteristics/Facts (related to example); Non-examples; Context (in which the word could be used).

VOCABULARY PROGRAMS	
Topic: High School—Mathematics, Statistics and Probability	
Step 5	**Self-Assess Your Plans and Progress with a Framework**
	Rigor/Relevance Framework: Are learning tasks moving students out of Quad A (low rigor/low relevance) and toward Quad D (high rigor/high relevance)?
	Rigor: Students are asked to comprehend mathematical vocabulary. The process of assigning imagery to definitions requires a number of high-level cognitive steps. They must apply their understanding of these words to imagine the kinds of visuals that could represent them. Once they have visual options, they will be required to make judgments about each to guide their image selection.
	Relevance: By customizing the Frayer Model, the teacher can make sure learning is relevant. Examples could include: The median price of apples on Freshdirect.com, which a competitor would want to know to determine how to price their own apples. The mean number of students in a school district who take the bus to school so that the district can determine how many busses it needs to transport all of its students. The mode in a school survey about students' favorite lunch option as selected from: pizza, vegetable salad, hamburger, tuna casserole, chicken noodle soup, pasta with meat sauce, and chili so that the school can plan lunches accordingly. The range of grades on a test so that a teacher can ascertain the breadth of understanding in her classroom.

The Frayer Model

The Frayer Model is a graphic organizer that is used to build vocabulary and analyze the meaning of words. It guides students through the process of defining a word, describing it or explaining its essential characteristics, thinking of examples of the word, and listing non-examples of the word.

The vocabulary word goes at the center of the model. In the definition space, students will define the word and note its part of speech. In the characteristics/facts space, students will write specific and identifying traits, features, and facts of the word to aid retention. In the examples space, students will affix their image or images. In the non-examples space, students will list antonyms, incorrect or inappropriate uses of the word, or images that represent non-examples (Frayer, Frederick, & Klausmeier, 1969).

A caveat for bold schoolers: to promote relevance, always customize the model to include a space for students to consider different contextual circumstances in which the word can be used. In this application space, students will list where else they think they might come across this word and why. The following example is a modified for relevance.

Frayer Model

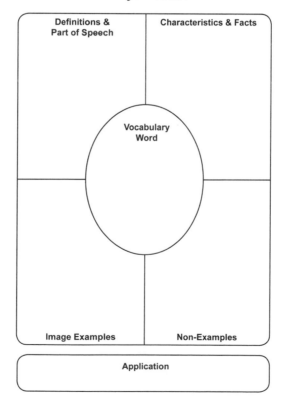

CHAPTER 6

BLENDED LEARNING
instructional strategy:
DIRECT INSTRUCTION

N ot all teachers are as lucky as Ben Stein in "Ferris Bueller's Day Off." In Chapter 4, we talked about how Ben Stein's character perfected the art of boring the crap out of his high school students. As he lectured in an almost impressive monotone, he fired off a stream of fill-in-the-blank questions. In response, his students fell asleep, drooled, and stared blankly back at him, as if catatonic from the insufferable drone of his lecture.

How do we know if our students are with us? That is the question. When it comes to direct instruction, tracking our students' levels of engagement can be the difference between OK and excellent direct instruction. Not one student in Ben Stein's classroom responded to any of his questions. But he didn't need their silence to know they were checked out.

They wore it on their faces. In a way, this made him lucky. It's not often we can accurately deduce from our students' faces if they comprehend as we lecture. Instead, we're too often left to make assumptions. Ben Stein was getting some pretty valuable feedback  from those sleeping students. Had he had a clearer understanding of direct instruction (and an ability to change the inflection of his voice), he would have been able to respond to that feedback, adjust instruction to meet his students where they were, and get some active participation out of them to push them all to mastery.

And this is the point. Direct instruction is more than lecturing—it's a choreographed, pre-planned series of events that come together to teach new information and support students through to mastery. In recent years, direct instruction has gotten a bad rap and fallen out of fashion. I think this is happened for a couple of reasons.

Firstly, I think this is because we got a little too excited about technologies. We got so distracted by the bright shiny objects that we left behind those things that felt dated by comparison. To many, direct instruction was one of those things. Next to those slick iPads, it looked dusty and cracked and tired . . . something to be left in the 20th century.

Secondly, it's often confused for lecturing. While lecturing is a part of direct instruction, it is not the whole enchilada. But because many people think direct instruction and lecturing are synonymous, direct instruction is often written off as a boring, low engagement didactic exercise. It's no wonder, then, that people often want to swap it out for the bright shiny objects.

The reality is that direct instruction is a multifaceted strategy with a strong .6 effect size (Hattie, 2008). There's more science to the art of direct instruction than might seem—a fact that is often forgotten. I'm going to tell you a secret: to be excellent at direct instruction, you don't have to be Kirk Daddow or John Keating from "Dead Poets Society." You don't have to get your kids standing on desks or clinging to your every word. What you need is a full-scale direct instruction plan. To achieve its .6 effect size, it must be done with intention, in alignment to academic goals, and include a few key components that help make sure you're connecting with students.

Exactly what direct instruction must include to achieve its potential varies depending on whom you ask. I prefer to go to the effect size master himself, Professor John Hattie. What follows is a summary of his outline of the necessary components of direct instruction:

- Prior to the class, the teacher identifies the academic intentions and the criteria for success, meaning what students will be accountable to learn and demonstrate.

- The teacher shares all expectations with students and gets confirmation that they understand the expectations of them.

- The teacher has a plan for the lecturing part of the class that includes modeling and checking for understanding.

- Students partake in guided practice while the teacher coaches students and provides remediation as needed.

- The teacher provides cues to students throughout when the most salient points are being made to help them synthesize and process information and form cohesive understanding.

- Students engage in independent practice to achieve mastery. The practice example should be related to, but different from the ones used up to this point in the class. (Hattie, 2015).

Even when direct instruction has all components in place, the challenge remains: How can we be certain that all of our students are following us as we lecture? How can we determine when it's time to move on or reteach?

Fortunately, most teachers are not Ben Stein-like in their style. Fortunately, most students are not as brazenly rude as the kids were in his classroom. Unfortunately, many of us still have no clue if all of our students are following us as we lecture. Trying to measure engagement and comprehension without breaking the flow or falling behind schedule is the great challenge of direct instruction.

Back when I broke Kirk Daddow down and convinced him to be my co-op teacher during pre-student teaching, he used to share his plan in detail before the start of every class. He would say, in effect, "I'm going to talk about this for about five minutes, then I'll move onto this for maybe three or four minutes. I'm not sure how long I'm going

to talk about the next topic . . . it's complex stuff, so we'll just see how well the students are getting it. I'll check in with them and decide if it's time to reteach or move on."

It's not uncommon to see some teachers not leave room for that last point—the possibility that the more difficult topics might necessitate some reteaching. Which might, in turn, cause a lecture plan to fall behind schedule, even get derailed—something most teachers don't like to let happen. It's also not uncommon to see teachers interrupt themselves during a lecture to ask their students if they're keeping up. It's not uncommon to see the majority of students nod their heads in agreement, almost as a reflex. Perhaps some are shy. Perhaps some don't want to be the person who interrupts class to ask for clarification. And perhaps most find it embarrassing to admit they're lost in front of classmates.

I cannot think of a better example of this than when I worked with high school English teacher Teddy. This man was another Kirk Daddow or John Keating, complete with all the stereotypical teacher trappings of sweater and tie, tortoise shell glasses, and chalk dust on his pants—always. His students adored him. He was recognized as the Fresno County Teacher of the Year, no doubt in part due for his incredible direct instruction classes.

Teddy faced just one problem: the strongest students gravitated toward his classes in droves, and they thrived in his classroom. As he lectured with enthusiasm and magnetism, Teddy would rely on visual cues to check to make sure everyone was with him. By all non-verbal accounts, almost all students were always with him. Yet, as I observed him, I kept my eye on the always-quiet students, wondering if they were intimidated in a class with so many thriving high achievers. Who wants to raise their hand in front of all the "smart kids" to admit they weren't getting something? These kids were listening, they were engaged, but they were poker facing their level of comprehension. They didn't want to invite Teddy to ask if they needed assistance in front of peers. I'd seen it a thousand times.

In my coaching experience, checking for learning tends to be the most challenging part of direct instruction. Historically, the tools available to teachers to check in with students throughout direction instruction, such as asking if everyone understands, bump up against the realities of dealing with humans. This is where modern technologies come in to save the day.

When it comes to direct instruction, technologies have opened up incredible opportunities for teachers to do a series of quick, formative assessments throughout a lesson to gauge comprehension. They're freeing students to use digital backchannels to let teachers know when they're off base or have questions—without breaking the flow of class and without having to raise hands and make a public confession of confusion. And they are, once and for all, solving one of direct instruction's most infamous sticking points: how to know if your students are ready for you to move on or are in need of further explanation.

This is exactly what we did in Teddy's class. We set him up with some backchannel technologies like TodaysMeet and Nearpod so that he could digitally and subtly communicate with those students too shy to speak up, but so happy to interact privately and in real-time with the teacher they loved. The technologies were a lifeline to these students. It was like releasing water from a dam; engagement flooded in. These kids who were once intimidated were now thriving—just in the way that made them comfortable.

Kirk Daddow and Teddy are proof positive that direct instruction is an instructional strategy worth hanging onto. Restoring direct instruction to its rightful place as an instructional strategy that *works* is bold school. As is layering it with some awesome technologies that will get you to that .6. To all of those who have declared direct instruction dead, I say: the reports of direct instruction's death have been greatly exaggerated. We just need to keep a few fundamentals in mind to make sure direct instruction achieves its potential and apply technologies to reach all students, all the time. Then we are all capable of being bold school masters of *blended* direct instruction, just like Teddy.

What those who've declared direct instruction dead need to learn:

1. *Direct instruction's greatest potential is when it's used to teach new knowledge.* Direct instruction packs its most punch when you

need to introduce new concepts to students. There are certain cases where new concepts are complex or nuanced enough that it makes the most sense just to explain them to students (Goodwin, 2011). In these cases, direct instruction should be a top contender for your instructional plans.

2. Direct instruction is multifaceted and intentional. For direct instruction to reach its .6 effect size, it must be purposeful, pre-planned, and possess certain components. Research has shown that when a teacher is transparent with the academic intent of direct instruction, it has a greater impact on learning (Goodwin, 2011). Effective direct instruction requires that the teacher model skills and check in with students throughout to make sure they're advancing toward learning goals. The teacher should also make it clear to kids when a critical point is being made. Guided practice should be included in any direct instruction class, as should the opportunity for independent practice so that students can work toward mastery.

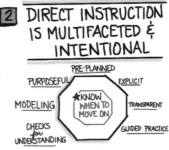

What matters is knowing when to move on. When to move on to guided practice. When to move on to independent practice. When to move on to a new topic in lecture. This is where technologies can elevate you to master of direct instruction status.

3. Technologies make monitoring student engagement and comprehension during direct instruction seamless, simple, and information rich. Several cool technology tools have come along that finally offer innovative solutions to the age-old challenge of direct instruction. Technologies offer two primary benefits that facilitate active student participation and assessment of comprehension during direct instruction:

a. *Technologies create backchannels of student-teacher communication.* Through tools like TodaysMeet and Google Slides, teachers and students can communicate 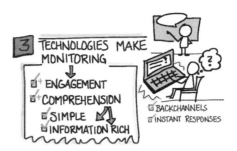 throughout direct instruction without breaking the flow. Such tools let students post questions as they have them, all without raising their hands. They can also expect that their teacher will address their questions before she has moved onto another topic and while a question is still fresh in mind.

b. *Technologies help teachers know when to stay and when to hit.* (Yeah . . . that's a blackjack reference in an education book. I'm fine with it.) So much of direct instruction is making assumptions about if your students are with you, if they're lost, if they're thinking about lunch. Thankfully, technology tools like Kahoot! and Poll Everywhere are taking the guesswork out of direct instruction. With Kahoot!, teachers can post a question with multiple-choice answers. Students answer via laptops or mobile phones. Instantly, the teacher can see the distribution of responses. Teachers can then decide if it's time to stay and spend more time clarifying a particular topic, or time to hit and provide students with new information.

If the Kahoot! data show answers that run the gamut, then it's likely that the concepts covered in the question are confusing to a good number of students. Stay. If most kids got the answer right, then it's fair to assume most comprehend what you've just discussed. Hit. If everyone

gets it right, you might want to consider upping the rigor. Hit again.

Kids love Kahoot! and the like. These tools bring a fun, game show-like element to direct instruction. Teachers tell me all the time they use Kahoot! because kids like it. What they might not know, though, is that the tool's secret weapon is its ability to deliver multiple, quick formative assessments. If you're going to use Kahoot! or Poll Everywhere, utilize it to its fullest extent. Let it not just be fun for your kids, but also inform your direct instruction pacing. It's here—where data drives decisions—that we become bold school masters of blended direct instruction.

———————

Taking a standard from elementary school social studies, let's plan direct instruction through the Bold School Framework.

**The Bold School Framework
for Strategic Blended Learning™**

DIRECT INSTRUCTION	
Topic: **Elementary School—Social Studies**	
Step 1	**Identify Desired Academic Outcome(s)** 1. Analyze cartoons, artifacts, artwork, charts, and graphs related to eras and themes. 2. Use and interpret primary source documents.
Step 2	**Select a Goal-Aligned Instructional Strategy That *Works*** *Direct Instruction* (.6 effect size) (Hattie, 2015) The teacher decides the academic goals of direct instruction and shares with them her students. Throughout the class, she demonstrates concepts and skills through modeling. She checks in routinely with students to assess their level of engagement and comprehension. Based on what is revealed in this assessment process, she makes a determination about whether or not students need further clarification on a topic or are ready for more material. Direct instruction classes must also include both guided and independent practice opportunities that use related, but different examples.
Step 3	**Choose Digital Tool(s)** *Kahoot!* Kahoot! lets teachers pose questions to students. The instantly generated answer summaries provide data that can guide teachers throughout direct instruction. Data can communicate that students comprehend the topic at a hand and it's appropriate for the teacher to move on. Or it can reveal that most students are in need of further clarification and it's time to reteach certain information. *Other strategic digital tool options: Google Slides, Poll Everywhere, Socrative, TodaysMeet*

DIRECT INSTRUCTION	
Topic: Elementary School—Social Studies	
Step 4	**Plan Blended Instruction**
	The teacher will use direct instruction to explain a methodology for interpreting political cartoons: identifying characters and purpose; identifying symbols; and interpreting symbolism for meaning. The teacher will then show students an example and provide additional direct instruction and modeling to demonstrate the process of interpreting the cartoon.
	The teacher will post a Kahoot! question specifically aimed at assessing students' comprehension (not recall) so far. Based on the answers, the teacher will stay and reteach or hit with new information.
	The teacher will then provide additional direct instruction around the political cartoon to place it within a historical context. She will then post another Kahoot! question and repeat the cycle.
	Once content has been fully explained and the teacher has confirmed that her students comprehend the material, they will partake in a guided practice exercise of interpreting a political cartoon. The teacher will float, answer questions, and deliver remediation as needed.
	Students will then engage in independent practice, this time interpreting other political artwork from the same era.
	The entire process will repeat as needed to cover all core topics and help students achieve mastery.

DIRECT INSTRUCTION *Topic:* Elementary School—Social Studies	
Step 5	**Self-Assess Your Plans and Progress with a Framework** *Rigor/Relevance Framework:* Are learning tasks moving students out of Quad A (low rigor/low relevance) and toward Quad D (high rigor/high relevance)? *Rigor:* Questions asked via Kahoot! should be aimed at comprehension, not recall. Therefore, questions should use verbiage that aligns with the higher orders of thinking in Bloom's Taxonomy. Question examples: • Determine the main character and/or idea in the cartoon. (Choose from a list of 4.) • Which of these items serves as a symbol in this cartoon? (Choose one from a list of 4.) • Which of the following statements do you believe best conveys the cartoonist's message? (Choose from a list of 4.) *Relevance:* Obvious opportunities for relevance in direct instruction come in the independent practice part of the class. It's important that students get to apply their skills in a way they understand, but to circumstances somewhat different from the practice done in class up to that point. Based on the age of the kids and the complexity of the class topic, teachers can make a judgment about just how different the independent practice example can be from those already used in class. Bringing relevance to elementary school history could be as simple as asking students to consider how they might apply these analytical skills to another discipline. Students could be asked in which other subjects might they use, analyze, and interpret primary source documents.

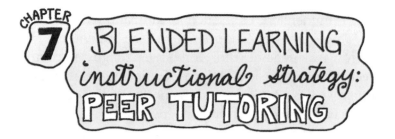

CHAPTER 7

BLENDED LEARNING
instructional strategy:
PEER TUTORING

With an effect size of .55 (Hattie, 2015), peer tutoring has been shown to have a gold mine of benefits when used strategically and with fidelity. In fact, it can unlock so many improvements and so much growth for both the tutor and the tutee that its biggest challenge is not how to do it, but how to do more of it.

Barbara's story is one of my favorites. I love it for a few reasons. When coaching Barbara, we had one of those true Quad D, SAMR Redefinition epiphanies. I love it because we took a strategy typically found in ELA classes and broke it out of that box. In Barbara's Spanish class, we were able to use technology at its finest, its most groundbreaking, and its most transcendent. And you can, too.

Foreign language teachers will be excited about this chapter because I know many of you feel there aren't enough strategies out there for you. While we will view peer tutoring through the lens of a Spanish class, this strategy can be applied to any class. In fact, that's the point of using a Spanish class, not an ELA class, to demonstrate peer tutoring—to show that this strategy can change the game in any discipline. So for you science teachers, math teachers, history teachers, PE teachers, music teachers—all teachers: with a dose of creativity and a layer of technology, this strategy can change the game in your classroom by breaking down walls and building up student growth in multiple meaningful ways.

Barbara had reached peak frustration. She, like any foreign language teacher, knew that the best way for a person to learn a language is immersion. To speak it, hear it, and write it with consistency. These three opportunities have to be present for a student to move toward fluency. In most foreign language classrooms, fluency feels like an unreachable goal. Typically, the teacher is the only fluent speaker in the room. It's not possible for her to converse with each student, all the time, every day.

As often happens in language classes, Barbara's instruction had devolved into the uninspired process of teaching vocabulary words and verb conjugation through memorization. Attempts to have her students converse in pairs proved unproductive, even counterproductive. The range of proficiency among her students meant that those who were stronger were slowed down by those who were less proficient. And those who were less proficient didn't know enough to point out errors in the speaking of those who were advanced. She resorted to having kids listen to and repeat conversations from recordings.

Barbara knew this way of learning language had little reward. But she was struggling to replicate the more immersive environment in her classroom she knew her students needed.

Enter peer tutoring. Or rather, enter one of those Oprah Aha! moments. With a flash of inspiration, everything changed for Barbara and her students.

Peer tutoring didn't work within her classroom walls. What if it worked outside of them?

Barbara, who now lived in Indianapolis, spent a year teaching in Mexico City. She reached out to a former colleague, also a foreign language teacher, there to see if he would want to team up and collaborate in international peer tutoring. It was an offer too good to refuse. Both teachers understood that by pairing their respective students, they could realize the dream of every foreign language teacher: an immersive environment—made possible through the miracle of technologies.

The Spanish-English peer tutoring program was born. For 12 minutes in every class, the students from

Indianapolis and Mexico City would hop on Skype and talk to each other. The U.S.-based kids would talk for six minutes in Spanish. And then the kids in Mexico would talk for six minutes in English. Prior to each "talk time," both teachers would give their students vocabulary they wanted them to focus on. The students were free to come up with the topic of conversation. Each offered critiques and corrections to their partners as they spoke.

Barbara and her counterpart in Mexico City saw their students' foreign language skills skyrocket, more than either had seen in their careers as teachers. The benefits, in scope and size, surprised them. Kids were retaining vocabulary (and we know why—they were learning it in conversational context rather than in a vacuum). The safety of speaking to a trusted peer, rather than in front of the class, let them grow more confident speaking in a non-native language. They were having fun and learning about a different culture. There was also an unexpected effect that took this peer tutoring to another level: the tutors got the incredible benefit of thinking deeply about their native language. Their grasp on their own language grew stronger, and they gained confidence through the act of helping newfound friends speak it with more proficiency.

Barbara's kids blossomed. And their ELA teachers took note, too.

The caveat to the international peer tutoring program was that it took all sorts of moving parts coming together perfectly. The time and class schedules for both classes had to line up just right. And they did. Until they didn't. Schedules got changed at the semester, and these classes no longer synced up for Skype calls. Kids in both cities were devastated. So too were their teachers, but they were also determined. They were not going to let go of a strategy so powerful just because of timing issues. So they decided to try out asynchronous communication.

Using the same approach, the students now simply recorded what they wanted to say to their talking buddy and sent it over to them, and vice versa. Then the kids

would listen to their talking buddy's recording, take notes, and provide feedback through an additional recording. And so on. The program was able to remain in place, just now via Voxer instead of Skype, and proficiency continued its upward climb in both Indianapolis and Mexico City. Bold school and Quad D 'til the cows come home.

There were some kinks to be worked out throughout the process, of course. As the program went on, Barbara and her colleague hit some speed bumps and found solutions, all in the name of making the program that much more bold school.

What Barbara needed to learn:

1. *Peer tutors must be matched intentionally so that it can be mutually beneficial.* There's a misconception out there that when we do peer tutoring, we should match the smart kids with the struggling kids. Part of the richness of peer tutoring comes from the safety and comfort it affords. It gives students a break from the natural intimidation of teachers. However, when the tutee knows they've been paired with someone seen as smarter, then the tutee still feels a degree of intimidation, as well as the potential for resentment.

Instead, peers should be matched on something they have in common, be it gender, proficiency, ethnicity, or socioeconomic status. Research shows that by forging partnerships on common social or academic achievement ground, the partnership will be safe to both participants and therefore more open and successful (Grubbs & Boes, 2009). In Barbara's case, she and her colleague matched students of comparable proficiency in each other's language.

There's another layer to this. This safety lends to trust. When the partners trust each other, the tutor will feel more comfortable giving feedback, and the tutee will feel more comfortable hearing it. The possible benefits here are enormous. This dynamic—two peers who can develop a mutually trusting partnership—has been shown to drive improvements in academics, self-esteem, attendance, motivation, behavior, and peer relationships. And not just for the tutee, but for the tutor, as well. The tutee feels supported by a trusted peer, and the tutor gains confidence through the role of acting as trusted coach and guide (Grubbs & Boes, 2009).

The movie "Finding Forrester" always comes to mind when I talk about the power of a mutually beneficial learning partnership. On a dare, a high school student in New York sneaks into the apartment of an older, reclusive man, about whom many myths and legends have been spread throughout the neighborhood. Thinking he was alone in the apartment, Jamal (Rob Brown) attempts to take a letter opener as proof to his friends, but is startled by the recluse himself, William Forrester (Sean Connery). In a panic, Jamal runs, leaving his backpack behind.

The next day, Forrester throws the backpack onto the court outside his window, where Jamal and his friends play basketball. Jamal, a gifted student and avid reader who dreams of writing books, discovers that Forrester made notes throughout his writing journal. Jamal is curious. He wonders if this person can help make him a better writer. After a few persistent knocks on Forrester's door, he relents and lets Jamal in—for the first of many visits.

At face value, the two have little in common. Jamal is an African-American kid from the Bronx. Forrester is an aging shut-in from Scotland who published a successful book decades ago and none since. Yet they both share a love for writing. On that bond, they develop a deep and mutually beneficial friendship. Jamal gains a writing tutor who helps bring forth his natural talents, which serves to change his future education and career prospects. And Forrester gains a trusted confidant, one who helps him grow comfortable opening up and leaving his house for the first time in decades.

Peer tutoring is most enriching and likely to succeed when both partners have something to offer the other. The mutual benefit between the Spanish and English speakers is obvious. Through purposeful peer matching, these benefits can be found in any discipline, even replicated across disciplines. It is not just for reading and ELA.

2. *Peer tutoring is for practice, not for teaching new skills or concepts.* Academic proficiency doesn't translate to teaching proficiency. It takes a specific skill set to bridge proficiency to non-proficiency. Those with these skill sets are called teachers. The teaching still needs to be the domain of teachers. Peer tutoring should be reserved for practicing learned concepts and skills.

3. *Peer tutoring only works if the tutors are trained in advance and teachers model tutoring skills.* Even though we're leaving the instruction to teachers, we are still dealing with students. We can't assume they have natural tutoring skills. Several studies have shown that peer tutoring programs won't move the needle in student achievement if the tutors aren't explicitly guided through what it means to be an effective tutor (Grubbs & Boes,

2009). The training needs to be relevant to the learning goals at hand as well, so that the tutor knows what to look for and address in the session.

4. *Peer tutoring is more effective when the students are in control.* A huge driver of the self-confidence and motivation gains is the agency students can assume in peer tutoring. When students have

control, they can practice making decisions, identifying and meeting needs, or expressing the need for help. The teacher's role is more of facilitator. In Barbara's class, she defined the academic goals, but then let the kids decide what they wanted to talk about and at what pacing. They controlled when they felt comfortable moving onto another topic or when one partner needed more practice.

5. *In addition to facilitating, the teacher needs to monitor and assess tutoring.* During peer tutoring sessions, teachers should be circling the room, looking over shoulders, and checking in with each pair. This supervision is vital to the success of peer tutoring (Grubbs & Boes, 2009). We are still dealing with children—it's up to us to be the adult in the room and make sure

they are staying focused and applying the tutoring skills they got in training. Peer tutoring also has the *added bonus* of freeing up teacher time to personalize instruction and deliver remediation as the tutoring takes place (National Education Association, n.d.).

Teachers should also be sure to build regular formative assessment into the program. We are being strategic here, of course. We're applying peer tutoring as a strategy to move students toward specific academic outcomes. Use an assessment tool that makes sense for your program to ensure this strategy is working as planned or to determine if it's in need of a review and refinement.

6. *The tutors do not need to be inside the classroom.* This is where blended peer tutoring changes the game. What Barbara and her colleague in Mexico City pulled off simply would not have been possible before internet technologies. Skype, Google Hangout, FaceTime … these technologies mean your students' tutoring partners can be anywhere in the world. Think outside the box here—or rather, outside the walls—and you can forge mutually beneficial partnerships in any school, city, even country for most any subject.

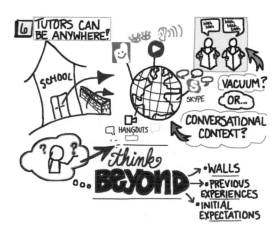

Keeping in mind what Barbara learned about making the most of peer tutoring, let's imagine the strategy used to partner middle school students with elementary school students for literacy learning through the Bold School Framework.

The Bold School Framework for Strategic Blended Learning™

PEER TUTORING	
Topic: **Middle and Elementary School—Literacy**	
Step 1	**Identify Desired Academic Outcome(s)** 1. Retell stories, including key details, and demonstrate understanding of their central message or lesson. 2. Describe characters, settings, and major events in a story using key details.
Step 2	**Select a Goal-Aligned Instructional Strategy That _Works_** _Peer Tutoring_ (.55 effect size) (Hattie, 2015) In this strategy, two peers are partnered based on shared circumstances or common proficiency needs (even in two disciplines, e.g., partnering a student strong in math and weak in science with someone weak in math and strong in science). All students are given tutor training in advance of launching the program. As needed, teachers model tutoring skills specific to the academic goals at hand, which are always shared with students. Teachers define the skills to be practiced in a tutoring session, and then leave most decisions (topic, pacing, evaluating performance, etc.) to the students for greater effect. The teacher instead focuses on monitoring the class and delivering remediation as needed.

PEER TUTORING	
Topic: **Middle and Elementary School—Literacy**	
Step 3	**Choose Digital Tool(s)** *Skype* Skype is a free app that lets people talk to others in any area code at little to no cost. For added benefit, video chat can be used so that students see their talking buddy and develop a more personal, trusting relationship. *Other strategic digital tool options:* Facebook, Google Hangouts, FaceTime, and Skype for synchronous conversations. Recap, ShowMe, Voxer, WhatsApp or any voice messaging tool for asynchronous conversations.
Step 4	**Plan Blended Instruction** Middle school and elementary school teachers partner to create a virtual reading buddy program in their schools or outside school if necessary. While in this particular case, the partners are not peers in a technical sense, they are matched on synergistic and aligned needs: the 1st graders, who are learning the fundamentals of literacy, partner with 6th graders, who are working toward improved literacy proficiency. The tutors (the 6th graders) are working to fill in literacy proficiency gaps, while the tutees (the 1st graders) are benefitting from guidance from someone less intimidating and more relatable than a teacher. The teachers of both the 6th grade tutors and the 1st grade tutees will devote some class time to delivering the concept or skills each wants her students to learn in their peer tutoring sessions. The 6th graders will have gotten formal and subject-specific tutor training at the start of the program. Before each tutoring session, their teacher will model how to coach tutees through practicing the next session's skills.

PEER TUTORING	
Topic: **Middle and Elementary School—Literacy**	
Step 4 *(cont.)*	The 6th graders will use tutor time to read to their 1st grade counterparts a Lexile® appropriate story that they have (ideally) not yet heard or read before. Once finished, the tutors will use question stems (provided by the 1st grade teacher, who has intentionally designed them to demand from students higher levels of cognition, not mere recall, to show comprehension). They will ask their elementary school tutees questions related to characters, setting, and events. At the conclusion of the tutoring time, the 6th graders will conduct a retell activity with their tutees.
	The 6th graders are responsible for reading with proficiency, using appropriate intonation, pacing, and discerning the accuracy of answers to the question stems. The entire activity can also be replicated asynchronously via the use of tools that allow for recording and message transfer (Recap, ShowMe, Voxer, WhatsApp).
	As the students engage in tutoring, the teachers in their respective classrooms will float, check in on all students, make sure they're staying focused, and offer assistance, remediation, or individualization as needed.
	After the reading time, both teachers will discuss with their students how the sessions went, address any questions that came up, and share discoveries, moments of new learning, and successes with the class.

PEER TUTORING	
Topic: **Middle and Elementary School—Literacy**	
Step 5	**Self-Assess Your Plans and Progress with a Framework** *Rigor/Relevance Framework:* Are learning tasks moving students out of Quad A (low rigor/low relevance) and toward Quad D (high rigor/high relevance)? *Rigor:* By serving as a tutor, the 6th graders will be thinking analytically about the tutee's comprehension skills. Since they are responsible for determining the accuracy of their tutee's answers, the tutors must evaluate their own comprehension and application of their understanding; it is a metacognitive exercise that demands that the tutor think both about the mechanics of comprehension and if their tutee is applying them. After evaluating the tutee's performance, the tutor will create specific, constructive feedback in a way that the tutee can understand. The tutees, on the other hand, are being asked to use listening and speaking skills. To ensure that this exercise is rigorous for the younger kids, the teacher must take care to construct question stems that demand higher levels of cognition in Bloom's Taxonomy, and not just recall or yes/no questions. The questions should seek to get the tutees to process, summarize, analyze, and evaluate the content being read to them.

PEER TUTORING	
Topic: **Middle and Elementary School—Literacy**	
Step 5 **(cont.)**	*Relevance:* As tutors, the 6th graders are required to apply their understanding and grasp of the mechanics of literacy to evaluating those of the tutee. It is a metacognitive exercise and a direct application of skills. Since the tutor will not know how their tutee will answer the question until they answer it, it is an unpredictable circumstance where the tutor will have to learn to be flexible and adapt his or her knowledge to help the tutee reach clarity and understanding. As tutees, the 1st graders are ideally hearing these books read aloud for the first time. As they listen, they'll respond to questions from their tutor that require them to process and synthesize the information so that their tutors can determine their level of comprehension. This skill of listening to information while simultaneously processing it and then recalling, synthesizing, and evaluating it as needed to answer questions is foundational to all reading that requires high levels of cognition. In that sense, these students are building the same skills they'll need to advance in literacy learning and future grades. It is also foundational to their ability to read and comprehend texts, articles, books, manuals, etc. outside of the classroom.

CHAPTER 8

BLENDED LEARNING
instructional strategy:
CONCEPT MAPPING

Greg was the graphic organizer king. When I first walked into his classroom, I counted 10 file cabinets, each filled with page after page of graphic organizers and worksheets. I come across teachers like this often. They will have all 180 days of instruction, student tasks, and worksheets planned, printed, and neatly organized in file cabinets on day one of the school year. And who can blame them? Teachers are overworked and overwhelmed. The Gregs of the world are just trying to stay ahead of the curve. Fair enough.

I don't fault teachers who organize as much of their school year as possible far in advance. In fact, I support pre-planning whenever possible. This is a book about pre-planning blended learning! We must remember, though, that pre-planning is only as good as it is aligned to academic goals.

Since I see so many Gregs, I was able to spot the break in his thinking immediately. The ultimate problem with Greg's approach was that it amounted—inadvertently—to teacher-centric instruction. This wasn't because Greg didn't care about his students; he absolutely did. He believed that his graphic organizers were effective tools for students to learn. He genuinely thought he was doing right by his kids.

With Greg, I knew we needed to change his thinking in one fundamental way, and then he *would* do right by his kids. The first day I began coaching Greg, he was teaching a class on persuasive writing. "Greg, what's your instructional strategy?" I asked him, knowing what his answer was going to be. Just as you probably do, too.

"This graphic organizer," he said, as he pointed to the day's worksheet.

That was the root of the problem. Graphic organizers are a tool, not a strategy. Classic goal-strategy-tool paradigm confusion. The first thing we had to do was straighten out his understanding of the paradigm so that he would no longer mistake graphic organizers for a strategy.

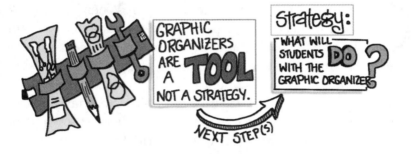

Graphic organizers can be great tools—when matched to a strategy and assessed through a framework to confirm that their use will move students toward an academic goal. But there is a truth to graphic organizers—a little known truth that can also be a little controversial.

The strategy is what kids *do* with the graphic organizer to build proficiency. The doing is the grappling, the thinking, the processing, the conceptualizing—the learning. All too often, graphic organizers are rigid and limiting. Take the classic hamburger paragraph graphic organizer. If this is a graphic organizer you utilize, take a deep breath and stay with me as you read what comes next. If you've never seen this graphic organizer before, congratulations.

Parts of a Paragraph

topic sentence

juicy detail #1
juicy detail #2
juicy detail #3

closing sentence

Keep this hamburger in mind every time you read a paragraph—in this book, in another book, in a newspaper. We know this isn't actually how people structure paragraphs. If every paragraph in every article or book you read followed this recipe, you wouldn't be able to read anything to the end. The robotic monotony of reading paragraph after paragraph like this would bore you into … turning on the TV.

Now this isn't to say that the hamburger doesn't have value. It's useful in helping kids think about the components of making a point in written form. But if we force every student into those sesame seed speckled buns, doesn't that seem a bit narrow? Don't we run the risk of locking their thinking into just one approach when we know that there are multiple ways to make a point in writing? Sometimes it takes only two sentences. Sometimes it takes two paragraphs, sometimes four. Sometimes it takes a whole article or even a chapter. Sometimes topic sentences are redundant, and sometimes the conclusion is better left unsaid.

This is the risk of relying on one graphic organizer to help kids ponder a concept; it leaves little room to ponder. It spoon-feeds too much information, and it presents just one way of thinking about something. If that one way doesn't resonate with a student, then they might not reach full understanding. We know that students learn by connecting two existing schema. This doesn't mean connecting to their teacher's schema; it means connecting to their own.

By the way ... don't you sort of want a hamburger now? Because I do. Aren't you a little distracted by realizing you're hungry? Now imagine you're 11 years old and presented with a visual of that hamburger! Mind now wandering into lunchtime ...

An alternative and more effective way to use graphic organizers is to present more than one to drive home the point that there are many ways we can think about ideas and concepts and that students should gravitate toward what works for them. Give students choice. Or better yet, let them create their own graphic organizer with a concept map.

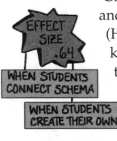

Concept maps are an instructional strategy in and of themselves, and with a solid .64 effect size (Hattie, 2015), for a very specific reason: they put kids in the driver's seat. The students are in control. They aren't locked into a particular graphic. Instead, they are free to create their own. Concept maps let students graphically represent their thinking in a way that makes sense to them. This requires that they think deeply about information and apply creativity to visualizing and mapping their understanding. Throw in technologies like Prezi or Popplet, and then kids have all kinds of ways to convey how they're connecting schema. Talk about letting your students be bold school.

Do you remember that 1998 movie, "Pleasantville"? Teenaged siblings David and Jennifer (played by Tobey Maguire and Reese Witherspoon, respectively) somehow get transported from their then modern day living room and into a 1958, black-and-white television show called "Pleasantville." The show was meant to be a typical, wholesome post-World War II sitcom. But to these kids who were coming of age in the MTV-ruled 1990s, this new suburban existence was bland, flat, and stale. Frustrated and disturbed by the lack of creativity, emotion, and diversity of any kind, David and Jennifer decide to introduce the townspeople to more modern ways of thinking and doing. They share with them provocative books, modern art, and novel ideas. These new perspectives liberate the minds of more and more people in the town. As they break free from the rigid customs and monolithic thinking of Pleasantville, they turn from black and white to color.

I often think of the transformation in this movie as the difference between the routine use of one limiting graphic organizer after another and the concept map. For students, the experience of repeatedly square pegging their thinking into the round hole of a provided graphic organizer is like learning in black and white. It's flat. It's dull. It's narrow. It's monotonous. And it's ineffective. The introduction of the concept map that they can control and design themselves in various technology tools is like the introduction of Technicolor. Learning is now varied, layered, unbound, of their creation, and full of possibilities. It's more effective and memorable. It's also bold school.

What Greg needed to learn:

1. *Graphic organizers are a tool, not a strategy.* When not used for its ability to advance a strategy, the graphic organizer isn't much different from throwing a technology tool into instruction just to say you did. If the graphic organizer wasn't purposefully chosen because it will help your kids meet a strategic academic goal, then there's no guarantee it will do anything to help students learn. There's a chance it might just waste time.

If you are going to use graphic organizers, make sure they will help your students develop the skills you want them to develop. And offer more than one so that they can choose the one that is most meaningful to how they think. When we don't differentiate our graphic

organizers, then instruction becomes about our choice, our preferences. It becomes about our desire for continuity, not about students achieving understanding and proficiency.

2. *Concept maps improve cognition and help students learn by putting them in control.* The brain achieves learning when it can connect a new idea to an old idea already coded in brain cells. Neurons (cells) in the brain literally make a synaptic connection and form a neural pathway when a person learns something. Therefore, making use of the existing schema is core to learning. When students are able to connect the new idea you teach them to one they already grasp, they are more likely to comprehend the new information. The more they reinforce this new understanding, the more reinforced that neural pathway gets, and the more likely they are to retain the concept (Arnold, 1997).

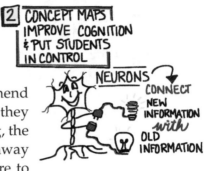

This is the brain science that explains why concept maps are such a useful instructional strategy, and there are reams of research that confirm their power. Concept maps give students the freedom to connect new information to existing schema in their brains for greater comprehension and retention (Rasmussen, 2015).

They also benefit students and teachers in other ways. Researchers from Boise State University and University of Illinois at Chicago were curious to know how much students understood about what they did and didn't know, otherwise known as metacognition. They divided seventh graders into three groups and asked them all to read passages of text. One group created their own concept map. The second was given a concept map to fill out. And the last group was asked just to read the passage twice. They were all then tested on the passage.

The researchers asked the students to guess how many questions they got right on the test. The kids who built their own concept maps were more accurate in their predictions. While those in this group didn't, on average, get more test questions right, they had a distinct advantage: in creating their own map, they were able to see exactly where their understanding was clear and where it was confused (Redford, Thiede, Wiley & Griffin, 2012).

The student-built concept map has the added effect of serving as formative assessment. It can show both teachers and students where a student might be struggling. Teachers can provide kids the specific remediation or coaching they need, and students can devote more time to studying and reflecting on those problem points.

3. *Leveraging technologies gives students that much more freedom to map their understanding.* The heart of concept maps' power is their capacity to take the shape of the connections made in a student's brain. Technologies bring that much more flexibility and dimension to the process of concept mapping and expand upon that power. Technology tools like Bubbl and Google  Slides allow for creativity that isn't limited by artistic ability in a way that pencil and paper cannot. When students are encouraged to conceive new ways to concept map, their thinking is that much more rigorous. When they are also encouraged to bridge the new information to what they already know—what is relevant to them and their worlds—the combination is pushing those students into Quadrant D of the Rigor/Relevance Framework.

4. *Concept mapping is three-step process that teachers model as needed so that students can eventually complete all steps on their own.* Concept maps are typically hierarchical, with the subordinate concepts stemming from the main concept or idea. This type of graphic organizer allows change and new concepts to be added. The Rubber Sheet Analogy states that concept

positions on a map can continuously change, while always maintaining the same relationship with the other ideas on the map.

With each step, begin by modeling it for your students. As they grow familiar with the competencies needed for each step, let them move through them in small groups. The objective is to coach students through to competency for each step so that they can, eventually, complete them all on their own.

> Step 1. *Start with a main idea, topic, or issue.* A helpful way to determine the context of your concept map is to choose a focus question—something that needs to be solved or a conclusion that needs to be reached. A predetermined topic or question will help with the hierarchical structure of the concept map.

> Step 2. *Determine the key concepts.* Find the key concepts that connect and relate to your main idea and rank them; most general, inclusive concepts come first, then link to smaller, more specific concepts. Free students to select a technology that best supports how they think and how they want to input these points into a digital concept map.

> Step 3. *Connect concepts by creating linking phrases and words.* Once the basic links between the concepts are created, add cross-links, which connect concepts in different areas of the map, to further illustrate the relationships and strengthen students' understanding and knowledge on the topic.

———————

Let's reimagine one of Greg's classes, broken free from the confines of one graphic organizer, and instead as a concept mapping class designed through the Bold School Framework.

**The Bold School Framework
for Strategic Blended Learning™**

CONCEPT MAPPING *Topic:* Elementary School—Science	
Step 1	**Identify Desired Academic Outcome(s)** 1. Students will use tools to discern between structure and function. 2. Students will develop a model to showcase the different structures of various plants and animals along with their functions.
Step 2	**Select a Goal-Aligned Instructional Strategy That *Works*** *Concept Mapping* (.64 effect size) (Hattie, 2015) The three-step strategy begins with the teacher instructing about a concept with an emphasis on central ideas rather than details. Students then create a concept map, or a graphical representational of a conceptual structure. They begin by choosing a focus question, with teacher support as needed. Then they determine the most salient points of the concept, which requires analyzing themes and interrelationships of subordinate concepts and synthesizing information within the concept at large. After using technologies to input these points into the map, students create cross-links between concepts in different areas of the map. The teacher models as needed to support students through gaining all competencies necessary to complete the steps on their own.

CONCEPT MAPPING	
Topic: Elementary School—Science	
Step 3	**Choose Digital Tool(s)**
	Prezi
	Prezi is a digital presentation tool that allows students to create a concept map in a way that expresses and supports their thinking.
	Other strategic digital tool options: Bubbl, Google Slides, Popplet
Step 4	**Plan Blended Instruction**
	The teacher delivers instruction of the central ideas of form and function and how the different parts/structures of plants and animals relate to different functions. Students then select an animal or plant for which they will design a concept map. The concept map will feature the organism in its entirety, along with branches to subtopics that visually demonstrate how the object can be broken down into separate structures with separate functions. Students will use Prezi to create concept maps that include images of an organism's parts, along with student-generated descriptions of their functions.
Step 5	**Self-Assess Your Plans and Progress with a Framework**
	Rigor/Relevance Framework: Are learning tasks moving students out of Quad A (low rigor/low relevance) and toward Quad D (high rigor/high relevance)?
	Rigor: To complete a concept map, students must evaluate the organism they choose, synthesize various pieces of information about it, and visually convey their understanding of how all this information relates and connects. The act of creating a map from scratch demands the high levels of cognition found in Quad B.

CONCEPT MAPPING *Topic:* Elementary School—Science	
Step 5 **(Cont.)**	*Relevance:* By definition, the act of creating a concept map requires that students consider new ideas in a way that is relevant to their existing schema. They are also learning a methodology that they can replicate in other classes and at home when studying new concepts, in general and specific to form and function. To drive home the relevance of the concept map, the teacher will ask students to consider how concept maps can be applied in other situations, guiding their thinking with pre-planned questions as needed. Can this methodology be used to evaluate structure and function in other disciplines? Might it be usable to evaluate structure and function in a poem or essay? Why or why not? In what careers might this methodology apply? Can understanding the structure and function of a hummingbird inform how an engineer designs a helicopter? Relevance will be achieved by pointing to the ways that evaluative and comparative thinking can show up in other subject areas and in the real world.

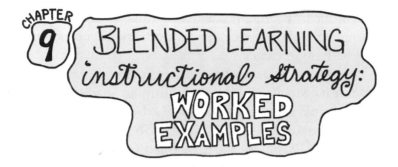

CHAPTER 9 BLENDED LEARNING instructional strategy: WORKED EXAMPLES

How do I say this . . .

Let me put it this way.

Have you seen "The Sandlot," the 1993 movie about the new kid on the block, Scotty Smalls, whose family moved to the San Fernando Valley in the summer of 1962? Smalls, as he's called, meets a group of middle school boys who regularly gather in the neighborhood to play baseball. In a desperate ploy to fit in with this crew, he swipes a ball from his stepdad's trophy case and the boys use it in their pick up game. Only when it's lost does little Scotty Smalls reveal that the ball was signed by none other than Babe Ruth. "The King of Crash, the Sultan of Swat . . . The Great Bambinooooooo!"

Among his new baseball buddies is the Michael "Squints" Palladorus, the slight, nerdy, bespectacled shortstop. Squints is obsessed with, awestruck, gob-smacked by the older, mature, beautiful Wendy Peffercorn, a high school student and lifeguard at the pool where the boys spend summers swimming—and gawking.

One afternoon, all the boys are in the pool, hypnotized by Wendy Peffercorn as she sits atop her lifeguard chair in a red swimsuit and applies what we can imagine is probably tanning oil (this is, after all, 1962). They float in the water, mouths agape, eyes popping out of their heads.

"I swim here every summer of my adult life," the young Squints says, as he defogs his glasses. "Every summer, there she is. Lotioning. Oiling. Oiling. Lotioning! Smiling! Smiling! I can't take this no more!"

Grammar transgression aside, Squints' inability to focus on anything but Wendy Peffercorn reminds me of a coaching experience I had a while back.

Kate, or Miss Stone as the students called her, was a middle school math teacher. She was teaching an introductory lesson on proportional relationships. I will be blunt. She had the blessing and the curse of being an undeniably attractive teacher in a middle school. Each time she turned to the board to do a worked example, I would look at the hormone-surged boys in her class and know exactly what they were thinking. After all, I have spent time as a middle-school boy myself. I could just hear their inner thoughts as she turned her back to them to model the problem. "Every day, there she is. Writing. Erasing. Erasing! Writing! I can't focus anymore!"

This is the fact of teaching students. Whether it's a teacher who distracts them, or the friend to their right whispering something, or a new Snapchat being surreptitiously viewed under the desk, or some noise from outside the window, students' attention is tough to gain and easy to lose.

We know modeling works. We know we need to do worked examples for students. But one of the problems of worked examples is that they typically get done a grand total of one time in a class. This means that 100 percent of your students have to have 100 percent focus as you do a worked example 100 percent of the time. We are dealing with kids here. This just isn't going to happen. Just about anything can easily derail the otherwise really strong worked examples strategy.

In the 2008 publication *Visible Learning*, John Hattie shared his research and synthesis of 800 meta-analyses of about 150 instructional strategies to calculate for each an effect size, and to determine which ones work best in the classroom. In 2015, he released an update to his research based on the addition of a few hundred more meta-analyses. In some cases, new research changed a strategy's effect size measurably. Full disclosure: worked examples is one of those. In 2008, Hattie gave it a .57 effect size. In his 2015 update, it was downgraded to .37 (Hattie, 2015). While there are still tons of studies that validate the potential of worked examples, I understand the downgrade. Because of the Wendy Peffercorns of the world—and multiple social media accounts and video games chipping away at our focus.

This decreased effect size correlates directly with our decreased attention spans (Statistic Brain, 2016). It makes sense that before kids were distracted by ubiquitous mobile technologies and social media and had somewhat longer attention spans, worked examples could hold more sway over learning. But that's not the world we live in anymore. Like most everything in our world, worked examples needs a digital upgrade.

I have seen digital worked examples drive real student growth. If you told me you were going to keep all your worked examples analog—done on the board just one time—then I'd say your time and your students' time is better spent with a different strategy. But since we're bold school blended learning masters, I say not so fast. While I don't (yet!) have the team to do a thousand-plus meta-analyses study of *blended* worked examples, I have been observing their use for years. As a blended instructional strategy, it remains powerful and worth folding into your instruction with regularity. On this one, you will just have to trust me.

The potential power of worked examples pertains to how the brain processes information. When a student's brain confronts new information, it quickly filters it through its sensory memory. The information that seems unimportant gets filtered out, and the information that seems important moves onto the working memory. It's in this part of the information processing model that the brain grapples with the information and tries to make sense of it. If the brain is able to connect existing schema or create new ones, then the brain attaches meaning to the new information. When this happens, the information can move onto the long-term memory (DataWORKS Curriculum, n.d.). Success!

The working memory is like the gatekeeper to retention. It's also pretty limited. Scientists refer to cognitive load theory to try to explain what limits and stresses working memory and what might cause information to fail to get moved onto long-term memory.

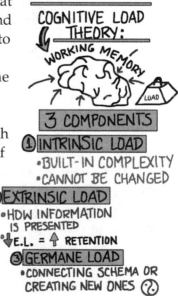

Three components make up the cognitive load theory of learning:

1. *Intrinsic cognitive load*, which is the inherent complexity of a concept or problem. Intrinsic load cannot be manipulated by the teacher; what a concept or task requires a student to process at one time is what it requires.

2. *Extraneous cognitive load* refers to information not related to the concept or problem but that is needed to understand or work through a problem. Teachers can influence extraneous load.

3. *Germane cognitive load* refers to the part of brain processing that is trying to connect schema or create new ones. Teachers also have the ability to affect germane load. Both intrinsic and extraneous cognitive load have a limiting effect on the working memory's capacity to process information. Germane load offsets some of that stress on the working memory by helping the brain connect schema (Paas, Renkl & Sweller, 2003).

When blended with technologies, worked examples work because they can help to reduce the extraneous load and increase the germane load students experience when they learn and practice new material. For digital worked examples to achieve this, they need two components: 1) The teacher needs to model a clear, step-by-step solution for how to solve a problem while also explaining the thought process; and 2) The teacher needs to point out the elements of the approach that serve to make the process more efficient (Paas, Renkl & Sweller, 2003).

Worked examples are trying to influence a pretty complex and fragile cognitive process. It stands to reason that one go at an analog worked example, especially when there are Wendy Peffercorns in the world, isn't going to cut it. It stands to reason that repeat exposure can lessen the cognitive load and help students move that new, complex information out of the working memory and into long-term memory.

This is where technology fits beautifully into the worked example strategy. This is one of those low-hanging fruit opportunities for bold school instruction. It's the difference of hitting record and not. Bold schoolers hit record.

There are multiple tools out there like ShowMe and Screencastomatic that allow you to record a worked example and then share it with your students. On tablets or laptops, kids can then review it as many times as they need to account for any

proficiency gaps or distractions that might happen in the classroom. Students get to set the pace that they need to achieve comprehension. By bringing in technologies, students can move on
when they are ready—not when most of the students in the class
are ready or when the teacher decides to move on. They can watch
and rewatch the example, hear the metacognition as the teacher
explains her step-by-step thought process, digest her strategies
and tactics, and really absorb the problem-solving path.

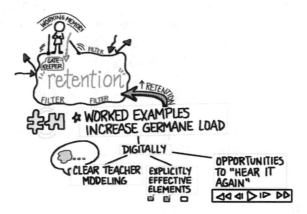

Blended worked examples help us deal with the realities of
teaching students: their minds are going to wander. But in doing
a strategically planned digital worked example and then handing
it over to students to rewind, fast-forward, and play again and
again, eventually, they will all get it.

You will see the power of digital worked examples immediately. Yet, if you really want to hit the ball out of the park (and
you do—you're bold school), their effect is maximized when alter-
nated with problem-solving opportunities. Several lab experi-
ments have confirmed that when students switch between studying worked examples and then attempting to solve a similar problem on their own, they learn more (U.S. Department of Education,
2007). One such study asked two groups of students to work with
12 statistics problems. In the first group, the conventional group,
the kids completed all problems as practice. The other group,
the worked examples group, were given eight problems worked

out for them and then were asked to solve the remaining four on their own. The worked examples group far outshined the kids in the conventional group; they spent less time studying the problem solving process and scored higher on a test. They also performed better with different kinds of problems that asked them to apply the principles they learned in the worked examples (Clark & Mayer, 2003).

Another study took it a step further, asking a group of algebra students to review one worked example, do a practice problem, review another worked example, do another practice problem, and so on. These students outperformed those who received all worked examples up front followed by all practice problems. This same research found that students who get the benefit of worked examples make fewer mistakes, can get through follow-up problems faster, and need less teacher help. By immediately applying what they learned by studying the worked example, misconceptions are broken down and understanding of concepts is reinforced (McGinn, Lange & Booth, 2015).

While this back and forth between worked examples and problem solving has been studied across a range of disciplines, the most profound impact has been found when used in math, science, and technology learning.

What Kate (and any teacher teaching kids) needed to learn:

1. *Worked examples need two components to be effective.* They require that the teacher outline a step-by-step process to solve a problem, while also specifically explain-ing the thought process behind it. The teacher also needs to be sure to explicitly point out those steps that serve to make the approach more efficient so that students can attach this new information to existing schema.

2. *Technologies must be leveraged to let students review a worked example as many times as necessary to understand and retain the concept at hand.* There are so many fantastic technologies out there that give you flexibility in going about solving a problem or explaining

a step-by-step process. Be sure to use one that  also allows you to record and share the recording with students in a format they all can use.

3. *Worked examples should alternate with practice problems.* I can't stress this point enough. Tons of studies show improved learning when students toggle between worked examples and independent problem solving opportunities. In fact, in an early classroom study, researchers compared traditional lecture-based math instruction to a class where lectures were mostly replaced by worked examples. The students in the worked examples classroom completed a three-year course sequence in two years, with test performance as good or better than the kids in the conventional math class (Worked example principle, 2009).

Convinced yet? Alternate between digital worked examples, where kids can set their own pace, and independent problem solving opportunities so students can immediately apply and reinforce what they've learned. Do this, and you will achieve bold school status as a worked example master.

Let's walk through a worked example using the Bold School Framework.

The Bold School Framework
for Strategic Blended Learning™

WORKED EXAMPLES *Topic:* Grade 7—Math, Proportional Relationships	
Step 1	**Identify Desired Academic Outcome(s)** 1. Recognize and represent proportional relationships between quantities.
Step 2	**Select a Goal-Aligned Instructional Strategy That *Works*** *Worked Examples* Worked examples begin with a problem statement and are followed by an explicitly stated step-by-step solution. The teacher takes care to point out those steps that increase the efficiency of the solution to help reduce cognitive load. For maximal impact, worked examples should be digitally recorded so students can set their own pace. And they should be alternated with independent problem solving opportunities for students so that they can immediately apply the principles they just learned.
Step 3	**Choose Digital Tool(s)** *ShowMe* The ShowMe app is a virtual and interactive whiteboard that lets teachers replicate the act of writing on a white board while also recording and broadcasting the process to students via a computer screen, smartphone, projector, and/or interactive whiteboard. In the app, which works well on tablets, the teacher uses his finger to write out steps and move through the solution. He can also bring in imagery and manipulate information. Key to this strategy, the tool turns recordings into screencasts that the teacher can then share with students. *Other strategic digital tool options:* EdPuzzle, ExplainEverything, Screencast-o-matic

WORKED EXAMPLES *Topic:* Grade 7—Math, Proportional Relationships	
Step 4	**Plan Blended Instruction** In lieu of working example problems on the board in front of the class, the teacher will record instruction in ShowMe and distribute content to be viewed asynchronously in a Learning Management System. At the onset of the recording, the teacher explains the concept of proportional relationships, stopping periodically to address academic vocabulary and pausing periodically to create meaning by connecting to existing schema. The teacher will continue by providing worked example problems in the ShowMe platform. Within the worked examples we will see and hear: a problem statement, colors and imagery to provide visual distinctions, step-by-step solutions. As the teacher walks students through the solution, he will explain his metacognition associated with the problem solving process and point out the tricks and tools that make the problem solving more efficient. Once done with the example, he will share the ShowMe video with students via an embedded link in Google Classroom. The students will be given time to replay the worked example as needed before moving onto a practice problem. The teacher, meanwhile, will float and assist students as needed, thus multiplying the opportunities for teacher-led instruction by two. Once students are done with the practice problem, they move to another asynchronous worked example embedded in Google Classroom and repeat the cycle. Or if necessary, the teacher can teach additional information and then repeat the cycle. The point being that students alternate between worked examples and practice problems as opposed to seeing a singular worked example live, and then using the duration of the class to work on practice problems.

\textbf{WORKED EXAMPLES} *Topic:* **Grade 7—Math, Proportional Relationships**	
Step 5	**Self-Assess Your Plans and Progress with a Framework** Rigor/Relevance Framework: Are learning tasks moving students out of Quad A (low rigor/low relevance) and toward Quad D (high rigor/high relevance)? *Rigor:* When teachers take care to explain their problem solving thought process, they are modeling the metacognition that goes into finding a solution. This naturally forces students to evaluate their own thinking in addition to the skills they are learning. By pushing problem solving out of merely a memorization and replication practice and into a metacognitive process, students will understand why a solution is or is not the most efficient and logical option. This robust level of thinking deepens learning, comprehension, and retention and also allows students to apply principles learned more flexibly to other topics. To achieve this level of rigor, teachers must make sure they talk through their process in detail while recording their worked examples. *Relevance:* Practicing metacognition will prime students to more readily connect learning to different domains. Because students are not just memorizing steps, they will begin to see for themselves how principles learned might apply to other areas within the content domain at hand or other disciplines entirely. As an example, a student who understands why she solved a statistical problem the way she did will be able to make connections to rates of occurrence in biology or sociology. Guide students towards making these relevant connections on their own by pointing out how what you're teaching can apply to other disciplines or real-world scenarios where fitting. Where possible, collaborate with teachers in other disciplines to extend relevance of core concepts.

CHAPTER 10 — BLENDED LEARNING instructional strategy: SELF-ASSESSMENT

I recently watched the "Bubble Boy" episode of "Seinfeld." And I realized something. This episode could not be made today. In this episode, George gets stuck playing Trivial Pursuit with the "boy"—who is very much a grown man and a surly, cranky one at that—who lives in a germ-protected bubble. Reading from the game card, George asks bubble boy, "Who invaded Spain in the eighth century?" Bubble boy answers with the Moors. But due perhaps to a smudge on the card, the card reads "Moops." The two cantankerous men argue back and forth: "Moors!" "Moops!" "Moors!" "Moops!" One quick smartphone Google search would have cleared that right up. Hell, insert Google Maps into the equation and Jerry and George never even would have met the Bubble Boy!

This made me wonder how many other plots would no longer work in today's interconnected, internet-centric, information anytime, anywhere world. Several classic episodes from "Seinfeld" alone would no longer work. Many of the show's plots rested on confusion and chaos that today could easily be cleared up with smart technologies.

Take the episode where Jerry, Elaine, George, and Kramer can't find their car in a New Jersey parking garage. They decide to split up, but then lose each other. After hours of aimless wandering, both George and Jerry have been arrested for public urination and Elaine is left to yell out for Jerry over and over in maddened desperation. A few text messages would have allowed them to reconnect within minutes of losing each other.

Thank goodness those treasures of the small screen were made when they were. And thank goodness we are teaching when we are. Because we are in a moment where technology creates gains, not losses, for what we do—when we use it the bold school way to triple down on the strategies that most positively impact kids, while letting technology elevate our instruction and enhance learning.

Self-assessment is one of those strategies that technology easily takes to the next level. Actually to the *next* next level, since this one is coming in hot at a 1.33 effect size (Hattie, 2015). Technologies have cracked open the potential for self-assessment in ways that weren't possible before them. If we have to lose some "Seinfeld" episodes because of the miracle of technologies, I say it's worth it.

Marisa loved exit tickets. She used them almost every day to get a sense of how well her students grasped the day's lessons. At the close of each class, her kids would fill out a quick worksheet and then place them on her desk on their way out. Every day that I was in her classroom, I'd watch her peer at the pile of papers before her and sigh. She loved exit tickets for the information they revealed to her, but she didn't love how they created more work for her. Every day, she'd have to go through all those tickets, log their responses, calculate any data, and make sense of the composite picture.

I asked Marisa if she would let me coach her through the process of turning her exit tickets into a self-assessment process for students. With its 1.33 effect size (Hattie, 2015), self-assessment is in an elite strategy that has the power to bring three year's worth of academic growth over one year's worth of time when used with fidelity. It's a no-brainer. Here's the good news: technology makes implementing this strategy in your classroom super easy. Here's the better news: the blended learning approach to self-assessment is a twofer; it's a self-assessment that can serve as an exit ticket all in one. As Elaine from "Seinfeld" would say, "Get out!"

But we're going to get into it. To do so, first we need to clear up some confusion around this strategy, specifically, its name. When John Hattie first titled this strategy, he called it "self-reported grades." He's since said that if he could write *Visible Learning* again, he'd rename this strategy "student expectations." I prefer to call it "self-assessment" (Cognition Education 2012). First, the strategy is not about students reporting their own grades; there's far more to it than that. Second, while helping students believe they are capable of meeting high expectations is an intended byproduct of this strategy, having self-expectations is not an academic skill. So with all due respect to the master himself, we're going to call it self-assessment. Because coaching students through the process of self-assessment is the heart of the matter.

It is also what pushes students to grow their expectations of themselves, stretch to meet them, grow them again, and so on and so forth. Research has found that when students have frequent opportunities to self-assess, they begin to attribute their learning to internal beliefs. In turn, they develop an awareness that they are in control. They come to understand that effort and the subsequent learning that comes from that effort, not luck or some outside factor, is directly connected to their success (Fernandes & Fontana, 1996).

I want to draw extra attention to that "subsequent learning that comes from that effort." What's important to remember is that we have to keep effort on equal footing with learning. Professor Carol Dweck, author of *Mindset: The New Psychology of Success*, introduced us to the power of the growth mindset and the perils of the fixed mindset—concepts we've

all become familiar with, but perhaps a little confused about. In recent years, she's worked to clear up some misconceptions about her mindset research and its fruitful, not empty, application. She reminds us that effort is a means to an end, and that the end is learning. While effort is key and deserves recognition, the point is learning, and it is the learning that deserves praise. Too often, Dweck has observed, educators are overly praising effort even in the absence of consequent learning. Confidence comes from learning, not effort. Or at least it should, if we are striving to nurture in our students substantive, lasting confidence, the kind that serves as a foundation for lifelong success and resilience (Dweck, 2015).

For the self-assessment strategy to turn newfound confidence and self-belief into improved outcomes, it has to be used within a larger, but simple cycle. We can't let self-assessments or exit tickets get lost in a vacuum. They must happen within a larger context that has a beginning, a middle, and an end. Something else has a beginning, a middle, and an end: a good story. Self-assessments, when used strategically, should tell a story—one of student progress toward proficiency.

In the beginning, the teacher needs to define for students what proficiency is and the benchmarks they'll be measured against as they move toward it. This sets up students to be active participants in their own learning. In the middle, students are given some sort of self-assessment opportunity, followed by a teacher-guided dialogue with students—individually or as a class (depending on what the circumstances warrant)—about the revelations of the assessment. At this point, students gain more control over their learning, as they now have awareness about what *they* need to change or do more of to meet benchmarks. In the end, students are given the chance, through some sort of learning task, to apply what they learned while reflecting on their assessment and make improvements. This is where those internal beliefs that students are in control of their learning get nurtured and reinforced. All told, we have a story about students who worked toward a goal; assessed and reflected on their progress; talked with the teacher about where they are and why; then got the chance to improve in practice. It's a happy story—that then starts over again.

Using this self-assessment cycle, Marisa and I took her offline exit tickets and put them online. In Google Forms, we recreated exit tickets in a way that could also serve as a robust, automated self-assessment tool for her middle school math students.

Marisa asked her students to demonstrate knowledge around fractions, pattern recognition, and story problems by using the following question. The student responses gave her a wealth of information about who was likely to need help and where they were likely to struggle.

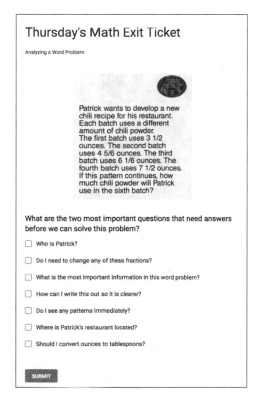

As students filled out the form, Google Docs automatically updated and calculated user data into a dashboard. While answers came in, Marisa monitored the dashboard to get a sense of how well her students understood the most fundamental aspects of the word problem.

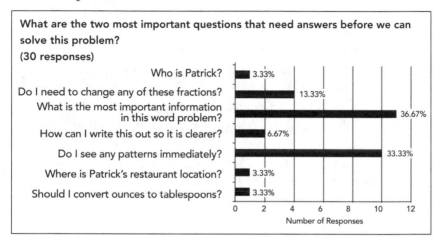

What are the two most important questions that need answers before we can solve this problem?
(30 responses)

Question	Percentage
Who is Patrick?	3.33%
Do I need to change any of these fractions?	13.33%
What is the most important information in this word problem?	36.67%
How can I write this out so it is clearer?	6.67%
Do I see any patterns immediately?	33.33%
Where is Patrick's restaurant location?	3.33%
Should I convert ounces to tablespoons?	3.33%

Number of Responses

This is where this tool cracks self-assessment wide open. Marisa authorized survey respondents—her students—to view the dashboard, as well. She set it so that all responses were anonymous. And boom: we have a twofer exit ticket and self-assessment strategy in just a few keystrokes. Not only does the teacher get information that informs her future instruction, the students also get the opportunity to measure themselves against the proficiency of their peers.

To understand why this becomes a self-assessment tool we just need to understand human nature. The first thing students do when they see this dashboard is measure how they stack up. Through this dashboard, students are able to compare their responses to those of their classmates and also see the range of answers given. Because we put this process in the larger self-assessment story cycle, students were aware of the proficiency benchmark they were being measured against and reflected on their performance accordingly.

We made one other big change to Marisa's exit tickets: we no longer had her use them exclusively at exit. Instead, she began incorporating self-assessment into class so that she could discuss the results with her students. Marisa still got the effect of an exit ticket, but in a way that let her deliver on the most important part of self-assessment—the chance for her kids to apply new awareness about their proficiency, or lack thereof. In discussing results with her kids, not only were they able then to measure themselves against the proficiency of the teacher, they were also able to discuss what they needed to do to improve.

What matters here is understanding that self-assessment isn't just a tool to paint a summative picture. It's a tool to act on. Self-assessment data should be used to inform instruction and keep all students meeting benchmarks and moving toward proficiency. It's a tool to nurture internal beliefs and encourage students to raise their expectations of themselves.

Thanks to the miracle of technologies, both Marisa and her students gained through the daily use of digital self-assessment cycles. Her students felt empowered by being brought into their learning. They felt more in control of their performance. They felt entrusted with and responsible for their own learning. And as an added bonus, Marisa found that by swapping out her exit tickets for digital self-assessments, she eliminated the time it took to go through the paper tickets and she saved time planning class. Each assessment provided information about what she needed to reteach and when her kids were ready to move on.

What Marisa needed to learn:

1. *Exit tickets are not a door to move onto the next lesson; they are a window into how to teach the next one.* Exit tickets are great—so long as they are used to inform the next day's (or even the next moment's) instruction. They are rich with potential data, for both students and teachers. Turn those exit tickets into a full-scale self-assessment cycle and everyone wins. Students get the benefit of self-assessing their proficiency, and teachers get the benefit of information that informs instruction.

EXIT TICKETS ARE A WINDOW

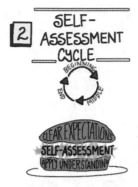

2. *Self-assessment has a beginning, a middle, and an end.* And then it starts again. In a way, self-assessment is the "Groundhog Day" of instructional strategies. If you watch that Bill Murray movie closely (and really, shouldn't we watch *all* Bill Murray movies closely?), you can see that his character, the arrogant weatherman Phil Connors, begins to change as February 2 remains on loop in his life. He begins to pay attention to how his behavior impacts people and affects his relationships. He gets the chance to correct mistakes and change his perspectives. And eventually, he comes to see the rewards of his progression toward being a softer, more thoughtful person.

This is our aim with the beginning, middle, and end self-assessment cycle: we use self-assessments sandwiched between clear expectations and the opportunity to apply understanding to move ever closer to those expectations. And then we repeat. Self-assessment is a feedback loop that never stops, nor should it because it has such potential to affect achievement.

3. *The power of assessment data comes from sharing it, not hoarding it.* The ability to share comes through technologies. In addition to Google Forms, Poll Everywhere, Kahoot!, and Twitter are tools great for quick self-assessment. The thing to keep in mind about Twitter is that there is, obviously, no anonymity. Yet, there are instances where the "end" of the self-assessment cycle is best served by allowing students to see what their peers said and who said it. Anonymity serves a purpose in the classroom, but beware of allowing students constant invisibility in their responses. Sooner or later, they need to take ownership of their work. They need to develop an understanding that their work is their signature, and that anonymity online is almost always a fallacy. This serves to promote 21st century competencies, while raising the quality of student work by pulling back the curtain of obscurity.

Now that we grasp the self-assessment cycle, let's go through a high school history class with the Bold School Framework.

The Bold School Framework for Strategic Blended Learning™

SELF-ASSESSMENT *Topic:* **High School—U.S. History, Revolution, and the New Nation**	
Step 1	**Identify Desired Academic Outcome(s)** 1. Compare and contrast differing sets of ideas, values, personalities, behaviors, and institutions by identifying likenesses and differences.
Step 2	**Select a Goal-Aligned Instructional Strategy That *Works*** *Self-Assessment* (1.33 effect size) (Hattie, 2015). Also called *Self-Reported Grades* or *Self-Expectations* Students are given the opportunity to self-assess their work and measure it against teacher explained proficiency and benchmarks. The teacher then discusses with students the results of assessment and helps each student grasp where they are relative to proficiency goals and what is needed to get there. Finally, students are given the opportunity to apply refined understanding to another learning task to see progress. The process exists as a cycle that is repeated with frequency for ultimate benefit to the student.
Step 3	**Choose Digital Tool(s)** *Poll Everywhere* Poll Everywhere is a tool that lets teachers ask students a question via the Poll Everywhere app. Students answer on a mobile phone, tablet, or computer. In real-time, responses can be viewed live online or in a PowerPoint. *Other strategic digital tool options:* Google Forms, Kahoot!, Twitter

SELF-ASSESSMENT *Topic:* High School—U.S. History, Revolution, and the New Nation	
Step 4	**Plan Blended Instruction** The teacher begins by clearly defining what proficiency for comparing and contrasting the Articles of Confederation and the United States Constitution looks like. She also explains the benchmarks that students will aim to meet and be measured against as they work toward proficiency. After the teacher sufficiently instructs on the concept at hand and the kids have engaged in practice or learning tasks as needed, they will have the opportunity to take a digital self-assessment. The teacher uses Poll Everywhere with an analogies-driven question for student self-assessment and so the teacher can ascertain her students' level of proficiency. Example: The Articles of Confederation is to the Constitution what _____ is to _____. a. A wheel is to car, because without one the other would not exist. b. A bee is to a flower, because both species need the other in the pollination process. c. All of the above. d. I have a different analogy. _____ is to _____ Students answer via the Poll Everywhere app on tablets and watch as the anonymous results upload to the app. After the teacher allows time for students to reflect on the assessment data and how they performed relative to peers and benchmarks, the teacher guides a discussion to analyze and understand the results.

SELF-ASSESSMENT *Topic:* High School—U.S. History, Revolution, and the New Nation	
Step 4 *(cont.)*	Based on the results, the teacher clarifies any misunderstanding and coaches students through the thought process needed to boost proficiency. She also uses the assessment data to inform her next stage of instruction, whether that is reteaching, further explanation of certain points, or moving onto the next topic. The self-assessment cycle repeats as needed.
Step 5	**Self-Assess Your Plans and Progress with a Framework** *Rigor/Relevance Framework:* Are learning tasks moving students out of Quad A (low rigor/low relevance) and toward Quad D (high rigor/high relevance)? *Rigor:* To ensure rigor when using self-assessment, the questions must speak to a student's level of comprehension, not mere recall. Be sure that self-assessment questions are asking students to think and demonstrate higher-order understanding. In the example question, the use of analogy requires that students first process and then compare information to other concepts. This evaluative process demands cognition high on Bloom's Taxonomy. *Relevance:* Analogies naturally get students thinking about how one concept does or does not pertain to another, if even in a small way. With analogies, relevance can be extended by carefully choosing the analogous options. In this example, an option about cross-pollination links learning to science and asks students to consider relationships that are one way or two way in another context. How else can you use analogies to link learning in your class to what students are learning in another class? How can you draw concepts to the outside world?

CHAPTER 11

BLENDED LEARNING instructional strategy: RECIPROCAL TEACHING

A h, reciprocal teaching. One of my favorite strategies. How do I love thee? Let me count the ways. First, it has a .74 effect size, so kids who experience reciprocal teaching frequently can get almost two years' worth of growth over one year's worth of time (Hattie, 2015). Second, based on the four cognitive literacy tools—prediction, clarifying, questioning, and summarizing—this simple strategy consists of what competent readers do without even realizing, which means this simple strategy can make competent readers of your students. Third, it's deceptively easy for teachers to implement, especially when technologies are involved, because the heavy lift is left to students. Fourth, it can be used in any discipline. Truly, any discipline. I once saw an art teacher use this strategy with a Van Gogh painting and a corresponding reading about the work. If an art teacher can use reciprocal teaching, so too can you. Even you, math teachers.

In addition to being one of my favorite strategies, reciprocal teaching is also one of the most misunderstood. There are two common misconceptions about reciprocal teaching that keep it from being used often and correctly. The first is that because it's a close reading strategy, it only makes sense in ELA classes. The second is that it's simply students teaching students.

Let's start by clearing up the first misconception. Reciprocal teaching is a close reading strategy, although I'm loath to call it that because this is part of what confuses people. It's one of many close reading strategies, one that happens to distill close reading down to a four-step cognitive process. But I ask you this: is ELA the only subject area where students have to read? Does

reading comprehension matter in math and social studies? Of course it does.

Students read in every discipline, and comprehension of what they read is necessary for success in that subject. Doesn't it make sense then that teachers of every discipline should consider themselves literacy teachers?

In 2006, the Successful Practices Network (SPN), a non-profit organization founded by Dr. Bill Daggett, used Lexile® Measures to compare 11th and 12th grade literacy requirements against the text demands of the typical entry-level employee, military personnel, and personal use. The study found that the reading requirements in these three areas were more rigorous than were 11th and 12th grade high school literacy requirements. SPN repeated the study nine years later to find that not only were schools still not preparing students for career-ready literacy, but also that the gap between school literacy and real-world literacy had grown (Daggett & Pedinotti, 2016).

For our students to gain the competencies they need for success in their lives, we must all consider ourselves literacy teachers. So we must all have an effective literacy strategy in our back pockets. With reciprocal teaching, you do.

Reciprocal teaching has been widely studied and widely validated for its ability to increase literacy skills. The research on its use in subjects other than reading or ELA is limited, but encouraging.

Researchers out of Australia decided to study reciprocal teaching in a middle school Human Society and Its Environment class (similar to what we in the U.S. would call a social studies class). The results were overwhelmingly positive. The benefit to the students who participated in the experiment extended beyond gaining content knowledge. They enjoyed the act of engaging in reciprocal teaching. The strategy made them more curious about the ideas they were reading. There was evidence that they internalized questioning and clarifying skills. Amazingly, these students changed their views of reading. It evolved from simply decoding text to grappling with the inferred meaning. The grand prize of takeaways? I'll leave it to the authors of the research report who said it best: "Most importantly, the [reciprocal teaching] process becomes a means of making literacy skills a major focus of education" (Cooper & Greive, 2009). Amen.

Now let's clear up the misconception that reciprocal teaching can be boiled down to something as rudimentary as kids teaching kids. Many teachers get this idea because in reciprocal teaching's most advanced iteration, teachers can have little involvement. Yet this can only happen once students have mastery over the four steps of the reciprocal teaching process. How can they get there, though, without us first teaching them? For reciprocal teaching to work, the teacher must be heavily involved at the outset. His involvement can only be scaled back once he's got evidence by way of student performance and formative assessments that his kids are ready to take on more responsibility in the reciprocal teaching process. But the teacher should always be monitoring and ready to remediate or assist as needed.

Now that we are clear on what reciprocal teaching isn't, let's get clear on what it is. Reciprocal teaching is a distinct four-step close reading process that must include opportunities for students to: 1) Predict, 2) Clarify, 2) Question, and 4) Summarize. When Palincsar and Brown designed this strategy, they determined that reading comprehension rested on six key points that they distilled into this four-step process (Cooper and Greive, 2009). The strategy is social and collaborative with students often working in groups of four or five. The students are constantly supporting each other and trading levels of responsibility, while the teacher monitors and makes sure each step is being approached appropriately and correctly. We have to remember that this process is challenging for a lot of students, particularly younger ones.

In the 1992 movie "A League of Their Own," a group of badass women step up to the plate, literally, to fill the shoes of soldiers at war and play professional baseball. Inspired by true events during World War II, the movie focuses on the Rockford Peaches, coached by Jimmy Dugan (played by the always perfect Tom Hanks)—a washed up, former marquee Cubs slugger who, at the start, treats this whole girls playing baseball thing as a joke. In the absence of his leadership, team leader Dottie Hinson (Geena Davis) guides her teammates the best way she knows how. It isn't great, but it's better than nothing. When Dugan finally realizes he's got some real talent on his team, he begins taking coaching seriously. With the guidance of a competent teacher, the team is unstoppable, and Dottie becomes the star of the league. When her husband unexpectedly returns from war, she decides to quit and return home to Oregon. Furious with her decision, as the team is moving ever closer to the World Series, Jimmy confronts her. Pleading with Dottie to stay, he says, "Baseball is what gets inside you. It's what lights you up."

"It just got too hard," Dottie says.

"It's supposed to be hard," Jimmy says. If it wasn't hard, everyone would do it. The hard is what makes it great."

I mention "A League of Their Own" not just because it gave us one of the best sports movie lines of all time ("There's no crying in baseball!"). I also mention it because when I explain reciprocal teaching to the teachers I work with, I emphasize both the reciprocity and the need for guidance from a master teacher before we turn the whole ballgame over to the students. In this strategy, there is this constant back and forth, back and forth of interaction and support—between teacher and students, between students and students. One person can't do it all. I compare it to a team sport, like baseball, where the teacher is the coach and the students are the players and everyone is working together toward the same goal.

Imagine a baseball practice. The coach is always there on the sidelines, guiding players as they practice different situations and techniques. The coach intervenes to correct errors and make suggestions. Meanwhile, as the players practice, one might hit the ball and make a run for first base. The shortstop fields the ground-ball hit, pivots and throws to second base to attempt an out on the player who just left first for second. The second 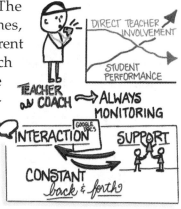 baseman catches the ball and then throws to first. There's constant movement and action. The coach continues to give directions and feedback. Given that these players are on the same team, they're all supporting each other toward improvement. Throughout the season, the coach might begin to take a more hands-off approach so that his players can grow more adept at applying skills and techniques on their own. But the coach will always remain vital and available to the team. Great coaches know that players perform at their best when communication is player-to-player, player-to-coach, and coach-to-player.

When we use reciprocal teaching, the same communication principles apply. We have to take care to support our students as they support each other. If we take ourselves out of the equation too soon (and there is no "Dottie Henson" sitting in the front row to lead the effort), students will 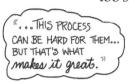 flail and the strategy won't drive its potential impact. While the bulk of our effort is facilitating student activities and engagement, it's important to keep in mind this strategy demands a lot of cognition from our students. This process can be hard for them. But that's what makes it great.

In my experience, reciprocal teaching is one of those strategies better shown than told. Let's go through a reciprocal teaching exercise in a 10th grade ELA class. Because we're bold school, we will of course be applying technologies to augment learning, nurture technology competencies, and make the reciprocal teaching process more efficient.

In this example, students will focus on *Night* by Elie Wiesel, the book they will soon start reading. First, the teacher must model the four steps of the process before turning it over to students.

Step 1: Predict. Students are given one minute to look at the front and back covers of the book and flip through the chapters. As a group, they make a prediction as to what they think the book is about and input it into a group Google Doc. They then have another minute to review the book again and make a determination as to whether or not they believe their prediction was accurate. As a class, students discuss their predictions and explain why they made them.

Teacher support: The teacher guides the class in a discussion about each group's prediction and why or why not it might be accurate. As students get more comfortable and competent with this process, the teacher can observe as the students discuss amongst themselves how accurate they think their predictions were and why.

Blended instruction: Each group creates a group Google Doc and types in their predictions.

Step 2: Clarify. Students then scan, but do not explicitly read, the first chapter to look for words they don't recognize or understand. They put their words into a shared class Google Doc, meaning that all students will work within the same Google Doc for this step. All words (or a selection of them if there are too many for this class period) from all groups are then assigned to groups to define.

For this step, we use the vocabulary strategy from chapter 5. Students use Google image search to look for visuals that represent the word or words they are defining. They then put them into a digital Frayer Model within a shared Google Doc so that all students can see all words' definitions, context, and associated imagery. The students then discuss within their groups and in the class the meaning of words.

Teacher support: With the guidance of the teacher, each group takes turns presenting the meaning, imagery, and context of at least one of the words they defined. As students improve, they can engage in this discussion with little to no teacher intervention.

Blended instruction: In this step, all students collaborate in a shared Google Doc that the teacher has embedded with as many Frayer Models as there are groups.

Step 3: Question. Once there is clarity around words, the students take turns within their groups reading the first chapter aloud (or silently if preferred). Then each group comes up with three questions, the foundations of which are scaffolded and provided by the teacher to make sure they achieve higher levels of cognition. Examples of scaffolded questions are:

1. A "right there" question, where the answer can be found directly in the text.

2. A "between the lines" question. For example, begin your question with, "In your opinion . . ."

3. A critical thinking question. For example, write a question that uses one of the newly learned vocabulary words.

The teacher then pairs all groups, and in these pairs, a group answers the other group's questions in the shared Google Doc and vice versa. Once done, groups discuss their answers with their partner group. The teacher then guides the class in a discussion about a selection of questions and answers.

Teacher support: The teacher checks on the questions students ask to make sure there is at least one from each group that is rigorous. He observes as the groups discuss their answers together and then leads a class conversation. As students gain competence, they can guide the class conversation, with the teacher intervening to clarify as needed.

Blended instruction: Students ask and answer questions in the shared Google Doc.

SUMMARIZE

Step 4: Summarize. Each group works to create a succinct summary of what the day's assigned chapter is about. Upon reaching consensus, they then live tweet the summary to the teacher. In this step, students are engaging in metacognition to reflect on the conversations and information they've gathered so far and distill it into a core takeaway. The class then discusses all the various summaries.

Teacher support: The teacher guides the class in a rigorous discussion about all groups' summaries as students read along on Twitter. Once students are fully competent in reciprocal teaching, they can lead this conversation on their own, with the teacher interjecting to maintain rigorous dialogue as needed.

Blended instruction: The students use Twitter to force succinct summarization that is also shareable with the class.

And there you have it. The back and forth and back and forth of this simple four-step process that yields huge cognitive growth. This is a strategy that can be used every one or two weeks. The more frequently it's used, the more comfortable your students get with it, and the more competent their literacy skills become.

As students grow more familiar with the reciprocal teaching process, they are given greater ownership over facilitating each of these steps. After all, our goal is two-fold: 1) To ensure kids comprehend the text and can interpret its meaning; and 2) To help students develop habituated behaviors around reading as an active endeavor whereby predicting, clarifying, questioning, and summarizing are omnipresent pieces of a larger puzzle.

What all teachers can benefit from learning about reciprocal teaching:

1. *Reciprocal teaching is for any discipline.* Reciprocal teaching can have a powerful impact on literacy and comprehension skills, and it cultivates deep and critical thinking skills. Students need to read and comprehend in every class. Therefore, this strategy fits into any subject and serves to

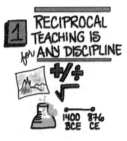

support students in all their classes, not just yours. Isn't that, after all, our ultimate goal as bold schoolers?

2. *The teacher must model all four steps of the reciprocal teaching process.* Since the reciprocal teaching strategy was introduced in 1984, scores of people have continued to study it. From a review of 19 such studies, it is clear that the strategy is much more effective when teachers first model the four cognitive steps (Rosenshine & Meister, 1993). And this doesn't mean once.

This means before every reciprocal teaching process—until you feel that all your students have mastered all four steps in the process. Only then can you begin to step back and transfer more responsibility to your students. But remember, you're the coach; you must always be on the sidelines watching your students, making suggestions for improvement, and correcting errors.

3. *Students do the questioning.* A common mistake I see is that in step 3, teachers provide the questions. The growth in this step happens when students come up with the questions. Yet, we will need to scaffold. If we leave this entirely to students, they will almost always draft questions that don't go beyond level one Bloom's.

4. *Let technologies deepen learning and make this process more efficient.* Reciprocal teaching is a seriously robust strategy, especially when technology allows you to bring in other blended instructional strategies. Since clarifying word meaning is so integral to this strategy and since we're bold school, we cannot let step 2, clarifying, devolve into looking up words in a dictionary. In step 2, let students use Google image search to find a visual for all vocabulary words to help retention.

Build a Frayer Model in a Google Doc so that they can put context around words and aid comprehension.

For the other steps, tools like Google Docs can make this process more efficient than pen and paper to ensure there's time to get through all steps. That said, we want to keep Allison from chapter 3 in mind. Remember how Allison piled on technology after technology in her interactive video class, most of which neither she nor her students knew how to use? Don't force technologies here just because you can. First make sure you and your students are comfortable using any tech tools that you bring in. If you have to choose one step for technology as you familiarize yourself with this strategy, make it for vocabulary words in step 2. Refer to chapter 5 to refresh on the blended vocabulary instructional strategy.

At long last, you are well on your way to becoming a bold school reciprocal teaching master—no matter what subject you teach. Let's now imagine what this could look like in a 5th grade math class using the Bold School Framework.

**The Bold School Framework
for Strategic Blended Learning™**

RECIPROCAL TEACHING *Topic:* Grade 5—Mathematics	
Step 1	**Identify Desired Academic Outcome(s)** 1. Make sense of problems and persevere in solving. 2. Use appropriate tools strategically.
Step 2	**Select a Goal-Aligned Instructional Strategy That *Works*** *Reciprocal Teaching* (.74 effect size) (Hattie, 2015) Reciprocal teaching is a 4-step, close reading strategy that uses the cognitive tools of: 1) Predict, 2) Clarify, 2) Question, and 4) Summarize. Critical to the success of this strategy is that the teacher spends time modeling each of these steps before students work through them on their own. As they do, the teacher must remain hands-on, guiding students and offering feedback and clarification throughout. The teacher only begins to transfer more responsibility to students once they can demonstrate mastery of the four skills. Even then, the teacher continues to observe students and offer support or remediation as needed.
Step 3	**Choose Digital Tool(s)** *Nearpod, Google Docs, Google image search, Google Classroom* Google image search allows students to find a visual representation of each vocabulary word. Using a Google Doc with a teacher-customized and embedded Frayer Model, students will be able to put each vocabulary word in context and enhance rigorous and relevant thinking. *Other strategic digital tool options:* Google Forms (for question creation), QR Codes (to access online math content), TodaysMeet (for summaries), Pear Deck (embedded questions and direct instruction)

	RECIPROCAL TEACHING *Topic:* Grade 5—Mathematics
Step 4	**Plan Blended Instruction** In this math class, students will solve a word problem. The teacher begins by breaking students into groups so that they can support one another throughout the reciprocal teaching process. The teacher uses Nearpod to share the word problem students will use, as well as the embedded questions and prompts at each step. *Step 1: Predict*—Students are given 15 seconds to scan a word problem on the screen at the front of the room and/or on their devices (programs like Nearpod and Pear Deck allow for both!). In their groups, they discuss what they think the word problem is asking them to solve and put their prediction into Google Docs. Students are then given the opportunity to scan the word problem again for another 15 seconds and discuss with their group if they expect their prediction to be accurate and why. The teacher then guides the class in a brief discussion about the predictions made and why or why not they were not accurate. *Step 2: Clarify*—The students then do another skim of the word problem to spot words they don't understand and list them in Google Docs. Students then use the vocabulary strategy in Chapter 5. For each word, they search in Google for a visual to represent the word and then put the word and image into a Frayer Model in Google Docs. The teacher then guides students in a conversation to ensure all students understand all new vocabulary words. *Step 3: Question*—Now that students comprehend all words in the math problem, they read it closely. They then come up with three questions, with scaffolding provided by the teacher to make sure they are rigorous, and put them into Google Docs. The teacher then assigns questions for each group to answer. Groups put their answers into Google Docs.

RECIPROCAL TEACHING *Topic:* **Grade 5—Mathematics**	
Step 4 **(cont.)**	*Step 4: Summarize*—Lastly, students solve the math problem individually or as a group and then summarize their process with their group. They create a one-minute video of their summary and post it to Google Classroom. The class then watches each group's video together (or a selection if each student has made a video), after which the teacher guides conversation about the differences and similarities of students' processes and what they might reveal.
Step 5	**Self-Assess Your Plans and Progress with a Framework** *Rigor/Relevance Framework:* Are learning tasks moving students out of Quad A (low rigor/low relevance) and toward Quad D (high rigor/high relevance)? *Rigor:* Because the teacher scaffolds question prompts, which were intentionally designed to encourage high levels of cognition, the questions will demand from students high levels of thinking on Bloom's Taxonomy. *Relevance:* Reciprocal teaching is a strategy that has a degree of relevance built in. In the process of going through the steps, students are applying new learning. To make the relevance of this process explicit to students, remind them that the cognitive process they're using is for reading for comprehension in general. Encourage them to use it every time they read, for every class, to the point that it becomes automatic. Clearly let them know that this process has the potential to make them more competent and skilled in all subjects.

CHAPTER 12 — BLENDED LEARNING instructional strategy: PROBLEM SOLVING TEACHING

When students walked into Alicia's 9th grade algebra class each day, they were directed to a warm-up problem on the board. While Alicia took attendance, the kids worked through the problem. On the day that I began working with Alicia, after giving her students a few minutes to solve the warm-up problem (that was never revisited), she began the day's lesson on factoring the difference of two squares. She demonstrated on the board how to go about an easy problem, including providing the formula and pieces of information the kids needed to know to solve the problem. She then solved the problem for them, step by step. She repeated this process for a medium problem and a hard one. Then she instructed her students to solve the odd problems on pages 63 and 64, giving them the rest of the class to do so. She told her kids to ask questions as needed, but few did. Instead, most just figured out how to replicate the problems she'd done on the board while flying below the radar.

Alicia shared with me that she genuinely believed she was using the problem solving teaching instructional strategy. Because in her mind, her kids were spending most of their time solving problems. I don't fault her for thinking this. There's a methodology that has emerged to teach math, and Alicia was following it to a T. What she, and so many other teachers, didn't realize was that in this approach, she is doing little more than spoon-feeding students the solution. She's doing all the effort and setting students up for nothing more than copying her work.

Author E. M. Forster famously said, "Spoon-feeding in the long run teaches us nothing but the shape of the spoon." This is absolutely true. When we spoon-feed information to students, we do the work for them. But the side effects go beyond merely handing students the solution. We rob them of all the long-term benefits of rigorous learning. We rob them of effort. We rob them of productive struggle. In turn, we rob them of opportunities to develop grit, perseverance, and resilience. We condition students to think that if they sit there long enough, someone will eventually come along and tell them the answer and how to get it. This is dull, passive, ineffective. It's not engaging, there's no rigor or relevance. And it's definitely not bold school.

Problem solving teaching has a stellar .63 effect size (Hattie, 2015), but only when it is purposefully used to let kids struggle and develop tenacity along the way.

So how do we let kids struggle productively as they solve all manners of problems?

One of the interesting things about problem solving in school is that we rarely present problems the way they present to us in real life. In real life, we stumble into a problem and then have to figure out how to solve it. We have to consider what information we're missing and need to gather before we can look for a solution. We have to determine which tools or resources we might need to solve it. Then we have to figure out how to apply these things to come up with a solution. When you think about it, it's the complete opposite of spoon-feeding.

For problem solving teaching to achieve its .63 effect size (Hattie, 2015), the problem solving must be authentic. It must look like what it looks like in real life. Problem solving teaching isn't about letting students solve a lot of problems on their own in class, following the steps you set out for them. It's about recreating in your classroom the circumstances of encountering an authentic problem.

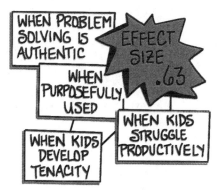

So let's do that. Let's increase the rigor and the relevance by designing authentic problem solving opportunities for our students. And let's use technologies as they can be used in the real world to support students as they figure out the best, most efficient solution to problems.

Authentic problem solving teaching is actually a simple and easy-to-follow five-step process:

1. *Model problem solving.* Note, I didn't say model the solution. Model the process of solving a problem. Show your kids that you begin by coming up with the essential questions that need answers to get started. Talk them through your process of evaluating and selecting resources or tools you need to solve the problem. Then articulate your thinking as you find the solution and solve the problem.

2. *Present students with a new problem.* It should be a problem similar to the one you modeled, but not so similar as to warrant a simple repetition of the steps you demonstrated.

We want this problem to allow students to struggle. In this struggle students develop the traits of a problem solver (perseverance, grit, and gumption) that will serve them well beyond the walls of your classroom.

3. *Have a class discussion.* Guide your students in a conversation about the initial considerations they need to make before they can begin solving the problem. Ask them what they think they need to know before getting started, encouraging them to come up with the essential questions, and steering them back on track when they veer far off.

4. *Set them free to problem solve.* Let students go about the resource and tool finding process on their own. Let them decide the formulas they need to solve the problem. And let them problem solve on their own, while staying available to provide support and guidance, but not solutions.

It's in this step that technologies come into play. In the real world, we use technologies to help us solve problems all the time. But we often feel hesitant to let our students do the same. We have the idea that it's somehow cheating or handing our students shortcuts. Let me pose this question to you: Isn't handing our students the exact steps and formulas to solve a problem so that they can replicate it over and over handing them the biggest shortcut of all? When we let students appraise a set of tools, evaluate what they do, and make judgments about which ones will help them find the most efficient solution, we are by no means handing them shortcuts. In fact, we're adding meaningful steps to their problem-solving process. We're making them think at high levels and ask essential questions, and then asking them to make decisions. We're encouraging persistence, perseverance, resilience, and a growth mindset. We're also giving them ownership over their learning.

I understand that there are some tools out there that could allow students to get the problem solved for them instantaneously. That's why you are still the smartest, most needed person in the room. It's up to us as teachers to provide a suite of technology tools and, as necessary, guidelines around their use. There's an awesome app out there called PhotoMath. This is one of those apps that reminds me we are living in the future, man. You take a picture of a problem on your phone and with the press of a button, like magic, it solves it for you. Talk about futuristic technology. Believe it or not, I encourage teachers to let their students use this tool—under guidelines. If PhotoMath is on the menu for the day, set a rule that phones or tablets are to remain at the top right of the desk until the final minutes of the class. Then they can use the app only to check for accuracy of the work they did to solve the problem.

As you begin this step, make your students aware of the tools they might want to consider using based on the problem at hand. Maybe it's a calculator. Or Google Sheets. Or PhotoMath. Maybe it's Geoboards or virtual manipulatives, both of which are powerful in that they let kids visualize mathematical concepts, numbers, or calculations. Stop short of telling them which tools make the most sense for the problem. Let them figure it all out.

This step works well both for individual students and students in groups. Another belief I often see in problem solving teaching is that if we let students collaborate to solve problems, no one individual will learn as much as they would on their own. However, the process of discussing a problem with others helps students think more critically about the steps to finding a solution. It can also help kids discover that problems can have more than one path to a solution (Vanderbilt University Center for Teaching, n.d.). We want to work toward students tackling the problem-solving process from start to finish on their own. But group work has its place and benefits on that road.

5. *Provide three rounds of spaced intervention:* 1) an initial intervention aimed at making sure students are on the right track; 2) an intermediate intervention to scaffold for those students who are still struggling; 3) a final, summative intervention in the last five or 10 minutes of class where we stop just shy of providing a step-by-step solution, but instead discuss the problem solving process as a class. At this point, I love to see students use a tool like Recap, where they record on phones, laptops, or tablets an articulation of their problem-solving process. The video exports directly to the teacher. I've seen teachers select a few to play for the class or invite the class to view each video in playlist form. The teacher then uses these recaps to structure a summative discussion on the possible and most efficient solutions to the problems the kids just productively struggled to solve.

What Alicia needed to learn:

1. *Problem solving teaching works best after surface knowledge has been mastered.* To get to its .63 effect size (Hattie, 2015), this strategy is best used for deeper learning. If it's used for new concepts before foundational knowledge has been mastered, it can lead to unproductive struggle. Make sure the concepts behind a problem have been well scaffolded and grasped by all of your students before moving to this strategy.

2. *Problem solving teaching means productive struggle within a structured process.* When it comes to problem solving, we learn and retain when we grapple with the different factors and possible solutions at hand. In the five-step process, kids are engaged and are thus more likely to remember what they learn, particularly compared to the rote, low-engagement process of simply replicating the steps a teacher laid out for them.

Vanderbilt University's Center for Teaching has done great research on this strategy. To help students get the most out of productive struggle, they emphasize being sensitive to the natural discomfort and lack of confidence learners might feel when left to tackle problem solving on their own. Provide positive reinforcement as they achieve little wins on the road to finding the solution. Communicate with them that the process is more important than the answer so that students feel supported going at the pace that suits them. By resisting the urge to give the answer, you are being patient with your students and modeling that they can be patient with themselves, too (Vanderbilt University, n.d.).

The five-step structure of problem solving teaching is the insurance policy to make sure that struggle remains productive rather than running off the rails to unproductive. It's the check to make sure kids don't get frustrated and discouraged to the point of giving up.

In the 1980 cult classic "Caddyshack," the self-important co-owner of a pretentious country club notices a gopher tearing up his golf course. He demands that the greenskeepers stop at nothing to get rid of the varmint. The nutty, oafish greenskeeper, Carl Spackler (Bill Murray) is put on the case. He tries all kinds schemes to kill the gopher. He tries to drown the gopher; the gopher escapes. He tries to kill it with a sniper; the gopher wins again. Eventually, he feels he has no choice but to create squirrel-shaped plastic explosives and drop them down the holes the gopher has chewed. The movie ends with most of the golf course in smoldering flames. . .while that dang gopher still survives and smugly dances to Kenny Loggins' "I'm Alright."

In problem solving teaching, we intervene because we don't want our kids to struggle to the point of failure. We do want them to look at the problem from multiple angles. We do want them to consider different possible solutions. We do want them to struggle—but productively. We don't want them to spin their wheels entirely on the wrong track. We intervene so that students won't, in effect, reach the point of blowing up the golf course. We want to guide them, point them in new directions as needed so that their cumulative experience when problem solving isn't failure.

3. *Embrace technologies, provide guide-lines.* A big objective of our instruction is that it is relevant to the world outside our classroom walls and that it arms kids with 21st century competencies. This has to include technology use that enhances learning and is real-world relevant.

Problem solving teaching is often the last place teachers look to add technologies, but, ironically, it's one of the most obvious. You use technologies all the time to solve problems in your work. It makes you more efficient and more precise. Let your students practice using problem-solving technologies to make them more efficient and precise. That is bold school. Put guidelines around technology use as needed to make sure students still go through every step of the problem solving productive struggle. And close learning with an exercise where they have to articulate their process to you or the class.

You are now well on our way to becoming a bold school master of coaching your students through the productive struggle of problem solving teaching. Let's now consider this strategy through the Bold School Framework.

The Bold School Framework
for Strategic Blended Learning™

PROBLEM SOLVING TEACHING *Topic:* Grades 6–12—Art	
Step 1	**Identify Desired Academic Outcome(s)** 1. Organize and develop artistic ideas and work. 2. Develop and refine artistic work for presentation.
Step 2	**Select a Goal-Aligned Instructional Strategy That _Works_** *Problem Solving Teaching* (.63 effect size) (Hattie, 2015) Problem solving teaching is an approach to problem solving where the focus is on the process of determining what's needed to solve a problem and how to go about finding the most efficient solution. When using this strategy, teachers should take care not to spoon-feed students formulas and all steps to solve a problem, but rather let them struggle productively to make their own evaluations and judgments. As both a rigorous and relevant approach to problem solving, this strategy is most effective for deeper learning and after surface knowledge has been mastered.
Step 3	**Choose Digital Tool(s)** *Minecraft and Screencast-o-matic* In the virtual land of Minecraft users can create their own worlds and experiences, using building blocks, resources discovered on the site, and their own creativity. The focus on creatively building and exploring helps build problem solving, planning, and organization skills. Screencast-o-matic allows users to record on-screen activity and create video clips. *Other strategic digital tool options:* Google Slides, Lego® Digital Designer

PROBLEM SOLVING TEACHING *Topic:* Grades 6–12—Art	
Step 4	**Plan Blended Instruction** Students will utilize Minecraft to design exterior structures and interior furnishings for fictional high-rise apartments in a city of their choosing. Designs must solve space constraint problems while also being visually pleasing and create fully functional living spaces. Students will then utilize screencast software to create virtual tours of their apartment and compare it to real apartments in the city they selected. Virtual gallery walks will allow students to show off their Minecraft creations. *Step 1:* Model some of the basic functionality that exists in Minecraft. *Step 2:* Present students with the Minecraft high-rise apartments design problem. *Step 3:* Discuss as a class the considerations, constraints, and requirements that students must take into account as they design (e.g., climate, space allocation, furnishings needed, etc.). *Step 4:* Set them free to problem solve and create, taking care not to provide any solutions for the students. Nurture productive struggle by letting them find solutions on their own, offering guidance when they've veered too far off course. *Step 5:* Provide three rounds of remediation spaced throughout the completion of the project.
Step 5	**Self-Assess Your Plans and Progress with a Framework** *Rigor/Relevance Framework:* Are learning tasks moving students out of Quad A (low rigor/low relevance) and toward Quad D (high rigor/high relevance)?

	PROBLEM SOLVING TEACHING *Topic:* Grades 6–12—Art
Step 5 *(cont.)*	*Rigor:* This is problem-solving task that relies heavily on creativity and evaluative thinking, where various options must be analyzed and measured against requirements and constraints. Ultimately students must make judgments based on the terms of the problems to be solved, e.g., working within space constraints while also seeking to achieve functional and visually pleasing designs and layouts. By definition, this task demands the high levels of cognition of analysis, synthesis, evaluation, creation, and originality. It's a meaty learning task, and one that could just as easily be used in a geometry, physics, trigonometry, or even basic algebra class with an added artistic and creative layer. *Relevance:* This problem-solving task also relies heavily on spatial-visual and logical-mathematical thinking. Encourage your students to bring in and lean on their math skills to help them conceive and calculate a layout that is realistic and reasonable. Be explicit about the convergence of the various skillsets that this task involves so that students understand the high level of relevance it brings. To drive home its real-world relevance, mention that this type of work is similar to what architects, contractors, interior designers, and landscape architects do. Mention that architects are always working within city codes and space constraints, such as construction constraints, land use constraints, and accessibility constraints, while briefly defining each. Explain that interior designers and decorators consider how to maximize the utility of an interior space while also considering both aesthetic and functional design.

CHAPTER 13
BLENDED LEARNING
instructional strategy:
SPACED vs. MASS PRACTICE

I n the movie "50 First Dates," Henry (Adam Sandler), a veterinarian at a Sea World-like park in Hawaii, takes an interest in a woman named Lucy (Drew Barrymore) he meets at a café. They talk, hit it off, and she asks Henry to meet her at the café again the next day. When he arrives the next morning, to his great dismay, Lucy has no recollection of him at all.

As it turns out, a year earlier, Lucy was in a car accident that left her with short-term memory loss. She wakes up every day thinking it's October 13, 2002, the day before her accident. Lucy's brother and father recreate this day for her every 24 hours, using a script and a newspaper with that date, to spare her the pain of confronting her memory loss again and again each day.

Eventually, she becomes hip to their stunt and upset that she is living a lie. Given that Henry likes this girl, he decides to make a video for her that explains her accident and how the two know each other. Every morning, Lucy watches this video so that she can try to start each day where she left off the day prior rather than where she left off on the day before the accident.

This movie always makes me think of the nature of teaching, at least one of its more maddening aspects: how by quarter two, what students learned in quarter one is fading from memory. By quarters three and four, it can be all but gone. We might spend a full week, even two, on one concept only to find that students have all but forgotten it just weeks or months later. Then we find ourselves wondering if we need to reteach, how much we need to reteach, and at the expense of what new content.

This was the frustration of Mark, a math teacher I worked with to help solve the problem of that student memory loss that snowballs with each passing quarter. Mark felt like he had so much content that he had to slog through that he was hesitant to devote time to content he'd already covered. But he could see that students weren't retaining key material weeks and months later, particularly those struggling students.

It has long been known that people retain information better when they are exposed to it regularly. Repeated retrieval of information boosts long-term retention. Retrieval that is spaced out over time also helps that information stick around in the brain for the long haul (Karpicke & Bauernschmidt, 2011).

How can we apply this fact of memory in our own classrooms? How can we realistically both focus on new content and also regularly pepper in the old content throughout the year to support and sustain retention?

It would have been nice if Mark could somehow start each class with some magically succinct, magically updated, and magically comprehensive video that kept all information covered to date fresh in students' minds. But this isn't Hollywood, this is real life! So we went with a solution that was feasible for Mark: the magical station rotation model.

We met the station rotation model in chapter 3 when we discussed the interactive video method. We've spaced out its mention . . . get it? Sorry, dumb joke. Actually, that is just a useful coincidence because the power of the station rotation model is that it can allow teachers to apply both spaced and mass practice in the same lesson plan.

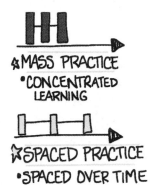

Spaced practice is that which is spaced out over some amount of substantial time and across the school year. Mass practice is practice where learning of a concept is concentrated for some shorter amount of time, perhaps days or a couple of weeks. Both have their utility and purpose. The good news is that the station rotation model doesn't make this a zero-sum game—we can do both spaced and mass practice simultaneously. The effect of using both in the station rotation model is that as students learn new material, they can go deeper into it to support comprehension, while also revisiting past concepts to support and sustain retention—all in the same class. When we make spaced practice a fixture of our instruction and student learning tasks, we can take advantage of its .6 effect size (Hattie, 2015).

To refresh, in the station rotation model, there are three stations set up in a classroom: 1) online instruction (in the case of chapter 3, it was interactive video); 2) teacher-led instruction; and 3) collaborative activities. New and old content can be divided among the three. Obviously, in most cases, the teacher-led instruction station will be dedicated to new content. Depending where in the instruction of new content you are, you can devote another station to new content and one to reinforcing older content or both to older content. You're bold school and your ultimate focus is doing what's best for your students. Let your judgment about where your students are and where you are in new content be the guide.

In this model, we don't have to lose entire classes or even entire precious chunks of time to reteaching. Not movie magic, but some serious teaching magic, and some seriously bold school magic at that.

What Mark needed to learn:

1. *Repeat exposure makes learning sticky.* To help our students retain what they learn while they're in our care, we have to play to what the cognitive research says, that repeat and spaced exposure to information enhances retention (Karpicke & Bauernschmidt, 2011). It's about more than just reteaching an old concept once; it's about exposing students to that older content multiple times, over time. When revisiting older content with spaced practice, be sure to let students engage with the material in different and cognitively rigorous ways each time so that they are not asked just to recall what they know, but show comprehension and an ability to apply the knowledge with flexibility. The more complex the learning task, the more space you should put between it and the next practice of those skills.

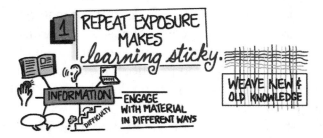

By creating space for spaced practice, we can repeatedly weave back in older information. In doing so, we avoid the problem of our students forgetting what was previously taught. In helping our students retain more, we are also helping them to know more. As the more we know, the more we *can* know because understanding and retention can only happen when two existing schema connect. The more one knows, the more schema she has to understand and retain new information (Arnold, 1997).

2. *Practice doesn't have to be either or; it can be both spaced and mass through the station rotation model.* By using the station rotation model to include both mass practice for comprehension of new material and spaced practice for retention of old material, we are freed from that conundrum of deciding to sacrifice time for new material to reteach old.

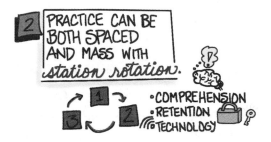

Imagine the station rotation model for a middle school social studies class on calendar notation. At station 1, you have an EdPuzzle interactive video to help students move through new material on B.C./A.D. vs. B.C.E./C.E. At station 2, you are guiding students through an exercise centered around placing events accurately on a timeline. And at station 3, your students could be taking a Google Forms quiz on previously learned content to reinforce previously learned skills, which provides proficiency data to you to inform future instruction.

The station rotation model is such a simple instructional strategy to apply. And it's such a simple way to serve both comprehension and retention at the same time. Keep in mind what we learned in chapter 3. While I will always recommend that at least one station include a strategic technology tool to enhance learning, don't get overzealous and throw in technologies at every turn. Particularly if you or your students are unfamiliar with the tool, and learning how to use it distracts from learning the content at hand.

———————

With the Bold School Framework as our guide, let's move through a spaced *and* mass practice in an ELA class using the station rotation model.

**The Bold School Framework
for Strategic Blended Learning™**

SPACED vs. MASS PRACTICE *Topic:* Grades 9–10—English Language Arts	
Step 1	**Identify Desired Academic Outcome(s)** 1. Refer to evidence from texts and other research on the topic or issue to stimulate a thoughtful, well-reasoned exchange of ideas. 2. Respond thoughtfully to diverse perspectives, summarize points of agreement and disagreement, and, when warranted, qualify or justify views and understanding and make new connections in light of the evidence and reasoning presented. 3. Draw evidence from literary or informational texts to support analysis, reflection, and research.
Step 2	**Select a Goal-Aligned Instructional Strategy That *Works*** *Spaced vs. Mass Practice* (.6 effect size) (Hattie, 2015) Retention is improved when exposure to information is repeated and spaced over time. In this strategy, we create opportunities for students to revisit older content in deliberate and purposeful ways to promote not just recall of that content, but also sustained comprehension of it. The more complex the practice is, the more space you should put between it and the next practice. By using spaced practice in the station rotation model, you can mix it in with mass practice of new content in the same lesson plan.

SPACED vs. MASS PRACTICE *Topic:* Grades 9–10—English Language Arts	
Step 3	**Choose Digital Tool(s)** *Recap and Google Forms* Recap is an online question and answer platform that allows students to assess and reflect. Google Forms allows teachers to create surveys, assessments, or web input forms. *Other strategic digital tool options:* Bing, EdPuzzle, Facebook Live, Google Docs
Step 4	**Plan Blended Instruction** At station 1, the teacher leads students through a small group discussion centered around the previous day's reading of "Who Speaks for the Animals." During this time, students use evidence from the text to reflect, analyze, and justify points of view while referencing the aforementioned content. At station 2, students view a persuasive argument on video via Recap discussing why the video's creator believes keeping exotic pets does not constitute animal cruelty. After listening to the narrator's perspective, students record a Recap response summarizing and explaining points of agreement and disagreement, and then submit the video to the teacher for feedback. At station 3, students engage in spaced practice. Revisiting a content piece covered earlier in the school year, students do a narrative quick write based on a prompt provided by the teacher and to continue to develop previously taught skills. Once the quick write is complete, students exchange work with partners in their group and engage in a collaborative editing and peer review using a rubric provided by the teacher in Google Forms.

SPACED vs. MASS PRACTICE *Topic:* Grades 9–10—English Language Arts	
Step 5	**Self-Assess Your Plans and Progress with a Framework** *Rigor/Relevance Framework:* Are learning tasks moving students out of Quad A (low rigor/low relevance) and toward Quad D (high rigor/high relevance)? *Rigor:* At station 1, rigor is achieved when the teacher intentionally pre-plans his questions and prompts to require that students use high levels of cognition. At station 2, students are thinking about and grappling with a real-world debate around what constitutes animal cruelty. They will need to incorporate what they learned from the reading (discussed at station 1), synthesize it with the arguments made in the video, evaluate all the information together, and arrive at specific judgments about a topic that is often more gray than black and white. They are also required to use evidence as they articulate and justify their opinions in their video presentation. At station 3, it's important that students are not asked just to recall a previously learned skill, but rather continue to apply the acquired skill. To make sure this is a rigorous task, learning prompts should require analysis, synthesis, and/or evaluation. Where applicable, ask students to grapple with information and content to make an evidence-backed judgment, as is the case in using a rubric to justify feedback of peer work.

SPACED vs. MASS PRACTICE	
Topic: Grades 9–10—English Language Arts	
Step 5 **(cont.)**	*Relevance:* To bring relevance to station 1, the teacher could ask students to think about the larger implications of a society that does not consider the humane treatment of animals. Students could also be asked to consider different industries where animal humanity and an avoidance of cruelty are relevant, e.g., the pet industry, food industry, cosmetic industry, zoos, etc.
	High relevance is achieved at station 2. Students are considering and responding to a real-world ethical debate, which requires that they not only think about the topic of animal cruelty at hand, but also its larger consequences on society. Ultimately, this topic is sometimes and somewhat ambiguous, just as most real-world issues are. Students are reckoning with arguments that come from many different voices with different perspectives and that do not always have one clear and definitive resolution—well capturing the unpredictable nature of such debates in the real world. This task also demands that students listen and speak in real-world ways. They are being asked to process and respond to information and formulate an evidence-backed assessment in ways that professionals do routinely in careers.
	In station 3, it's important that each spaced practice of prior skills is different from the last. Students not only need to keep skills fresh, they also need to keep them flexible. Each time you engage in spaced practice, come up with a new way for students to use the skills so that their ability to apply them becomes versatile and relevant to multiple scenarios, ideally including at least some real-world scenarios.

AFTERWORD

love pop culture and movies. In case you hadn't noticed. (It's why I started podcast called *Teaching Keating*, where my co-host and I use moments from movies and television as a springboard to talk about best practices in education.)

When I started this book, I knew I wanted to loop in memorable bits and pieces from pop culture to both illustrate points and make this book enjoyable for you. After all, we know that learning is more engaging when it can be joyful. As I began thinking about which movies to fold in, the first movie that came to mind was "The Shawshank Redemption." Confused about how Shawshank and blended learning mix? You made it this far; stick with me.

As fate would have it, I could find no natural home for this movie in any of the chapters. But I refuse to close this book without bringing in its beautiful lesson on commitment to goals, persistence in achieving them, and staying true to what we know matters.

If you haven't seen the movie, I'll begin by challenging you to re-evaluate your life choices. In the interim, here's a synopsis. Andy Dufresne (Tim Robbins) is wrongfully convicted of a crime and finds himself forced to adjust to the harsh realities of prison. As a banker in his former life, Andy offers his financial services to the captain of prison guards who is in need of tax advice. This affords him transfer to working in the prison library, which not only suits the intellectually curious Andy, but also keeps him safe from the violence he confronted while working in laundry.

Andy finds a library in decay and with limited books. As a person who appreciates the arts, he begins writing a weekly letter to the state government for additional library funding for more books. Andy imagines a library that can serve as a refuge where prisoners can come, read books that liberate their minds and transport them to other worlds, and benefit from the healing nature of words. Like any good teacher, Andy also knows that literacy is freedom, hope, and a future—something he hopes he and his fellow inmates can have.

Year after year, Andy writes one letter a week to the government. Until six years later, a shipment arrives to his attention with a letter from a state government official that reads:

"Dear Mr. Dufresne,

In response to your repeated inquiries, the state has allocated the enclosed funds [of $200] for your library project. In addition, the library district has generously responded with a charitable donation of used books and sundries. We trust this will fill your needs. We now consider the matter closed. Please stop sending us letters."

"Good for you, Andy," says a guard.

"It only took six years. From now on I'll write two letters a week instead of one," Andy says.

I love this story. It has always moved me. His persistence is steady, patient, focused, and unwavering. After six years of weekly letters, he finally gets a response. Yet he knows that his fellow inmates could benefit from even more funding and resources. So he remains persistent, aware that he can do better and do more for the education and futures of those around him.

Please keep this story in mind as you become a bold school blended learning master. Or if it doesn't resonate, keep in mind any story—from your world, a movie, a book, anything that inspires you. Stay resolute, committed, undeterred. Stay confident, focused on your goal, aware that it's a goal that matters. Stay hopeful. Remember there is no failure, only feedback. Don't let setbacks or mistakes discourage you. If we do, there will be no progress or growth anywhere, for us or our students. Show them what resilience looks like. Be an inspiration to them.

Persistence pays off. And in our case as educators, it pays off in spades—as it opens up hopeful, productive, prosperous, and bright futures for our students. What could matter more?

APPENDICES

The following tools and resources are mentioned explicitly or referenced in a chapter. For context on each appendix and how to use a given tool in blended instruction, please revisit the chapter listed where it has been explained or referenced. I've also included my current list of the most powerful tech tools that will help you elevate your instruction and enhance student learning and how technology aligns to each quadrant of the Rigor/Relevance Framework®.

Appendix A—The Bold School Framework for
Strategic Blended Learning™
Explained in Chapter 2; referenced in Chapters 3 through 13

Appendix B—Rigor/Relevance Framework®
Explained in Chapter 2; referenced throughout

Appendix C—Rigor/Relevance Framework® and SAMR
Explained in Chapter 2

Appendix D—Station Rotation Model
Explained in Chapter 3; referenced in Chapter 13

Appendix E—Verb List by Quadrant
Explained in Chapter 3; referenced throughout

Appendix F—The Frayer Model
Explained in Chapter 5; referenced in Chapter 11

Appendix G—Question Stems by Quadrant
Referenced in Chapter 7

Appendix H—Technology Use by Quadrant

Appendix I—Weston's Top 30 #EdTech Tools

Appendix A—The Bold School Framework for Blended Learning™

A GUIDE	
Step 1	**Identify Desired Academic Outcome(s)** 1. What skill or skills do I want to cultivate in students? 2. What priority standards will be addressed in this lesson?
Step 2	**Select a Goal-Aligned Instructional Strategy That *Works*** 1. What high effect size instructional strategy or strategies will I leverage to meet the academic outcomes above? 2. What will my students be doing in this lesson? (e.g., Concept Mapping .64) 3. What will I be doing in this lesson? (e.g., Direct Instruction .60)
Step 3	**Choose Digital Tool(s)** 1. What digital tool or tools can I use to elevate the chosen high effect size strategy? 2. How will these tools make me more efficient and effective? 3. How will the tools elevate or increase the rigor or relevance of student learning? 4. Will these tools allow me to double down on instructional strategies where I am my most skillful, or will they be a distraction to me, or my students?

A GUIDE	
Step 4	**Plan Blended Instruction** 1. How will I plan this lesson strategically with rigorous and relevant academic outcomes in mind? 2. What will I be doing and what will the students be doing throughout the class?
Step 5	**Self-Assess Your Plans and Progress with a Framework** *Rigor/Relevance Framework:* 1. Are learning tasks moving students out of Quad A (low rigor/low relevance) and toward Quad D (high rigor/high relevance)? 2. *Rigor:* Do questions or learning tasks require that students use the higher levels of cognition in Bloom's Knowledge Taxonomy? Are students evaluating, synthesizing, analyzing, and/or creating content? 3. *Relevance:* Will students be able to apply newly acquired knowledge across disciplines and/or to real-world predictable or unpredictable situations? Will students grasp that their learning is relevant to circumstances beyond the class content at hand?

Appendix B—Rigor/Relevance Framework®

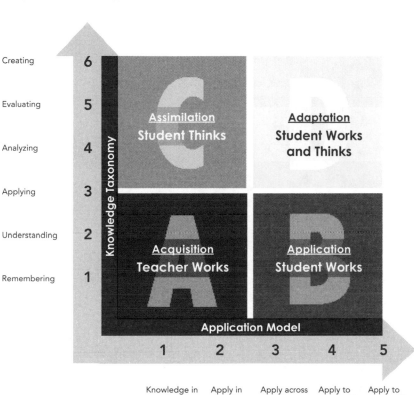

Creating   6

Evaluating   5

Analyzing   4

Applying   3

Understanding   2

Remembering   1

Knowledge Taxonomy

Assimilation
Student Thinks

Adaptation
**Student Works
and Thinks**

Acquisition
Teacher Works

Application
Student Works

Application Model

1   2   3   4   5

Knowledge in
one discipline

Apply in
discipline

Apply across
disciplines

Apply to
real-world
predictable
situations

Apply to
real-world
unpredictable
situations

Appendix C—Rigor/Relevance Framework® and SAMR

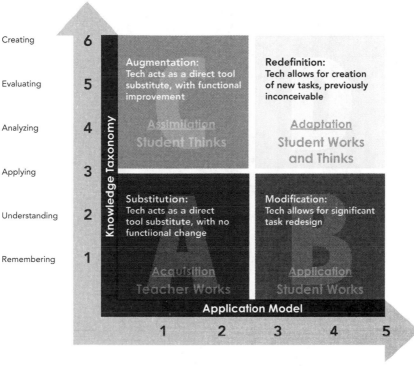

Creating   6

Evaluating   5

Analyzing   4

Applying   3

Understanding   2

Remembering   1

Knowledge Taxonomy

Augmentation:
Tech acts as a direct tool substitute, with functional improvement

Redefinition:
Tech allows for creation of new tasks, previously inconceivable

Assimilation
Student Thinks

Adaptation
Student Works and Thinks

Substitution:
Tech acts as a direct tool substitute, with no functiional change

Modification:
Tech allows for significant task redesign

Acquisition
Teacher Works

Application
Student Works

Application Model

1   2   3   4   5

Knowledge in one discipline | Apply in discipline | Apply across disciplines | Apply to real-world predictable situations | Apply to real-world unpredictable situations

Appendix D—Station Rotation Model

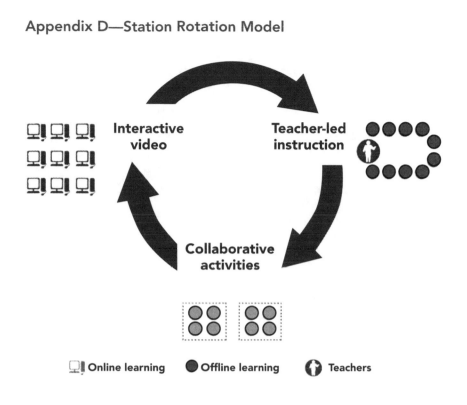

⬜ Online learning   ● Offline learning   ⓧ Teachers

Appendix E—Verb List by Quadrant

Use the Verb List by Quadrant to define the level of rigor. You can use this list to either create a desired level of expected student performance or to evaluate the level of existing curriculum, instruction, or assessment.

Quadrant A	Quadrant B	Quadrant C	Quadrant D
Calculate	Adjust	Analyze	Adapt
Choose	Apply	Categorize	Argue
Count	Build	Cite	Compose
Define	Collect	Classify	Conclude
Describe	Construct	Compare	Create
Find	Demonstrate	Conclude	Design
Identify	Display	Contrast	Develop
Label	Dramatize	Debate	Discover
List	Draw	Defend	Explore
Locate	Fix	Diagram	Formulate
Match	Follow	Differentiate	Invent
Memorize	Illustrate	Discriminate	Modify
Name	Interpret	Evaluate	Plan
Point to	Interview	Examine	Predict
Recall	Look up	Explain	Prioritize
Recite	Maintain	Express	Propose
Record	Make	Generate	Rate
Say	Measure	Infer	Recommend
Select	Model	Judge	Revise
Spell	Operate	Justify	Teach
View	Play	Prove	
	Practice	Research	
	Produce	Study	
	Relate	Summarize	
	Role-play		
	Sequence		
	Show		
	Solve		

Appendix F—The Frayer Model

Frayer Model

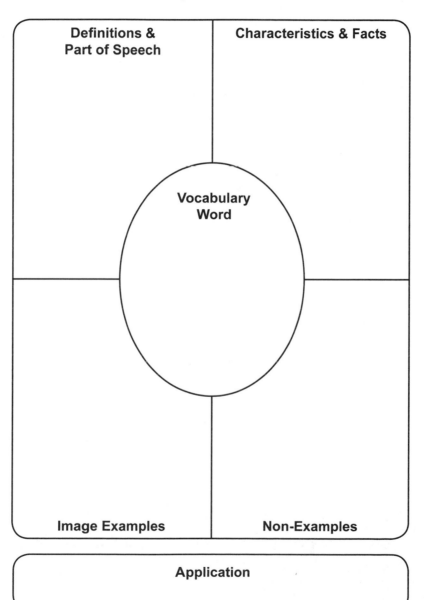

Definitions & Part of Speech	Characteristics & Facts

Vocabulary Word

| Image Examples | Non-Examples |

Application

Appendix G—Teacher Question Stems by Quadrant

In your learning environment, try using the following question stems that align to each quadrant. This can help move students toward increased rigor and relevance.

C

Ask questions to summarize, analyze, organize, or evaluate:

- How are these similar/different?
- How is the main idea supported by key details in the text?
- What's another way we could say/explain/express that?
- What do you think are some of the reasons/causes that ___ ?
- Why did _____ changes occur?
- How can you distinguish between _____ ?
- What is a better solution to _____ ?
- How would you defend your position about _____ ?
- What changes to _____ would you recommend?
- What evidence from the resources support your thinking?
- Where in the text is that explicit?
- Which ones do you think belong together?
- What things/events lead up to _____ ?
- What is the author's purpose?

D

Ask questions to predict, design, or create:

- How would you design a _____ to _____ ?
- How would you rewrite the ending to the story?
- What would be different today if that event occurred as _____ ?
- Can you see a possible solution to _____ ?
- How could you teach that to others?
- If you had access to all the resources, how would you deal with _____ ?
- How would you devise your own way to deal with _____ ?
- What new and unusual uses would you create for _____ ?
- Can you develop a proposal that would _____ ?
- How would you have handled _____ ?
- How would you do it differently?
- How does the text support your argument?
- Can you describe your reasoning?

Ask questions to recall facts, make observations, or demonstrate understanding:

- What is/are _____ ?
- How many _____ ?
- How do/does _____ ?
- What did you observe _____ ?
- What else can you tell me about _____ ?
- What does it mean to _____ ?
- What can you recall about _____ ?
- Where did you find that _____ ?
- Who is/was _____ ?
- In what ways _____ ?
- How would you define that in your own terms?
- What do/did you notice about this _____ ?
- What do/did you feel/hear/see/smell _____ ?
- What do/did you remember about _____ ?
- What did you find out about _____ ?

A

Ask questions to apply or relate:

- How would you do that?
- Where will you use that knowledge?
- How does that relate to your experience?
- How can you demonstrate that?
- What observations relate to _____ ?
- Where would you locate that information?
- Can you calculate that for _____ ?
- How would you illustrate that?
- How would you interpret that?
- Who could you interview?
- How would you collect that data?
- How do you know it works?
- Can you show me?
- Can you apply what you know to this real-world problem?
- How do you make sure it is done correctly?

B

Appendix H—Technology Use by Quadrant

Empower students to consider the following examples of technology use by quadrant.

Quadrant C	
• Editing	• Reverse
• Hyperlinking	Engineering
• Media	• Software
Clipping/	Cracking
Cropping	• Testing
• Monitoring	• Validating
• Photos/Video	Resources
• Programming	

Quadrant D	
• Animating	• Mashing–
• Audio Casting	Mixing/
• Blog	Remixing
Comments	• Networking
• Broadcasting	• Photo/Video
• Collaborating	Blogging
• Composing	• Podcasting
• Digital	• Reviewing
Storytelling	
• Directing	

Quadrant A	
• Bullets and	• Internet
Lists	Searching
• Creating	• Loading
and Naming	• Typing
Folders	• Using a Mouse
• Editing	• Word Doc
• Highlight–	
Selecting	

Quadrant B	
• Advanced	• Replying–
Searching	Commenting
• Annotating	• Sharing
• Blogs	• Social
• Google Docs	Bookmarking
• Operating/	• Subscribing to
Running a	RSS Feed
Program	• Tagging
• Posting–	• Texting
Social Media	• Uploading
	• Web Authoring

Appendix I—Weston's Top 30 #EdTech Tools

1. **G Suite**—(Google Drive, Docs, Slides, Sheets, Forms, Classroom, Sites) Everything, anytime, anywhere
2. **Poll Everywhere**—Live, interactive audience participation
3. **TodaysMeet**—Backchannel discussions
4. **Prezi**—Non-linear presentations and concept mapping
5. **Kahoot!**—Game-based feedback
6. **Popplet**—Capture and organize ideas
7. **Voxer**—Asynchronous conversation/discussion
8. **Socrative**—Quizzes, quick questions, and polls
9. **Vizia**—Integrate quizzes, polls, and CTAs into videos
10. **Remind**—Small and large group mobile communication
11. **ShowMe/Explain Everything**—Create and share tutorials
12. **PearDeck**—Interactive slide presentations
13. **NearPod**—Interactive slide presentations
14. **EdPuzzle**—Create interactive video content
15. **Canva**—Simple graphic design
16. **Screencast-O-Matic**—Create and share screen recordings
17. **Plickers**—Collect real-time data with a single smartphone
18. **Write About**—Writing prompts and resources
19. **Recap**—Create and share video
20. **GoFormative**—Live look at student screens
21. **Flippity**—Turn spreadsheets into flashcards
22. **Quizizz**—Multiplayer classroom review and assessment tool
23. **StoryBoard That**—Online storyboard creator
24. **Powtoon**—Create animated video
25. **Thinglink**—Annotate images and video
26. **iMovie**—Produce and edit video content
27. **Survey Monkey**—Create and publish online surveys
28. **Storybird**—Create publications to share and print
29. **Vocaroo**—Online voice recording
30. **Padlet**—Collaborative workspace

Arnold, C. *Read with Me: A Guide for Student Volunteers Starting Early Childhood Literacy Programs*, September, 1997. Retrieved from www2.ed.gov/PDFDocs/readwith.pdf

Clark, R. C., and R. E. Mayer. *e-Learning and the Science of Instruction: Proven Guidelines for Consumers and Designers of Multimedia Learning.* Jossey-Bass. 2003.

Cognition Education (Producer). (2012, May 2). Self reported grades with John Hattie [Video file]. Retrieved from vimeo.com/41465488

Cooper, T., and C. Greive. "The effectiveness of the methods of reciprocal teaching as applied within the NSW primary subject human society and its environment: An exploratory study." *TEACH Journal of Christian Education*, vol. 3, no. 1, 2009, pp. 45–52. Retrieved from research.avondale.edu.au/teach/vol3/iss1/11

Daggett, W. R. "Rigor/Relevance Framework®: A Guide to Focusing Resources to Increase Student Performance," 2016. Retrieved from leadered.com/pdf/Rigor%20Relevance%20Framework%20White%20Paper%202016.pdf

Daggett, W. R., and J. A. Pedinotti, Jr. "Reading Skills and the Career Readiness Gap," 2016. Retrieved from www.leadered.com/pdf/Reading_Skills_and_the_Career_Readiness_Gap_2016.pdf

DataWORKS Curriculum. "The Information Processing Model: A Primer On How Students (and All Humans) Learn," n.d. Retrieved from dataworksed.com/blog/2014/07/the-information-processing-model/

Dweck, C. "Carol Dweck Revisits the 'Growth Mindset'." *Education Week*, September 22, 2015. Retrieved from www.edweek.org/ew/articles/2015/09/23/carol-dweck-revisits-the-growth-mindset.html

Frayer, D., W. C. Frederick, and H. J. Klausmeier. *A Schema for Testing the Level of Cognitive Mastery*. Wisconsin Center for Education Research, 1969.

Fernandes, M., and D. Fontana. "Changes in Control Beliefs in Portuguese Primary School Pupils as a Consequence of the Employment of Self-Assessment Strategies." *British Journal of Educational Psychology*, vol. 66, 1996, pp. 301–313. doi:10.1111/j.2044-8279.1996.tb01199.x

Gilbertson, A. (Host)."The LA School iPad Scandal: What You Need to Know NPR Morning Edition, August 27, 2014.

Goodwin, B. *Simply Better: Doing What Matters Most to Change the Odds for Student Success.* ASCD. 2011.

Grubbs, Natalie, and S. R. Boes. "An Action Research Study of the Effectiveness of the Peer Tutoring Program at One Suburban Middle School," 2009. Retrieved from files.eric.ed.gov/fulltext/EJ871911.pdf

Hattie, J. "The Applicability of Visible Learning to Higher Education." *Scholarship of Teaching and Learning in Psychology*, vol. 1, no. 1, 2015, pp. 79–91. Retrieved from dx.doi.org/10.1037/stl0000021r

Helgoe, L. "Revenge of the Introvert." *Psychology Today*, September 1, 2010. Retrieved from www.psychologytoday.com/articles/201009/revenge-the-introvert

Hirsch, E. D., Jr. "Reading Comprehension Requires Knowledge of Words and the World: Scientific Insights into the Fourth-Grade Slump and the Nation's Stagnant Comprehension Scores." *American Educator*, Spring 2003, pp. 10–29.

Kamenetz, A. The Inside Story on LA Schools' iPad Rollout: "A Colossal Disaster." *The Hechinger Report*, September 30, 2013. Retrieved from digital.hechingerreport.org/content/the-inside-story-on-la-schools-ipad-rollout-a-colossal-disaster_914/

Karpicke, J. D., and A. Bauernschmidt. "Spaced Retrieval: Absolute Spacing Enhances Learning Regardless of Relative Spacing." *Journal of Experimental Psychology: American Psychological Association Learning, Memory, and Cognition*, vol. 37, no. 5, 2011, pp. 1250–1257. Retrieved from learninglab.psych.purdue.edu/downloads/2011_Karpicke_Bauernschmidt_JEPLMC.pdf

Klein, K. "L.A. Unified School District Doesn't Need More iPad Yes Men." *The Los Angeles Times*, May 23, 2014. Retrieved from www.latimes.com/opinion/opinion-la/la-ol-school-ipad-bond-20140523-story.html

Kouyoumdjian, H. "Learning Through Visuals: Visual Imagery in the Classroom." *Psychology Today*, July 20, 2012. Retrieved from www

.psychologytoday.com/blog/get-psyched/201207/learning-through -visuals

Kuhn, M. R., and S. A. Stahl. "Teaching Children to Learn Word Meanings From Context: A Synthesis and Some Questions." *Journal of Literacy Research*, vol. 30, no. 1, 1998, pp. 119–138. Retrieved from journals.sagepub.com/doi/pdf/10.1080/10862969809547983

McGinn, K. M., K. E. Lange, and J. L. Booth. "A Worked Example for Creating Worked Examples. *Mathematics Teaching in the Middle School*, August, 2015. Retrieved from www.nctm.org/Publications/Mathematics-Teaching-in-Middle-School/2015/Vol21/Issue1/A-Worked -Example-for-Creating-Worked-Examples/

National Center for Education Statistics. "The Nation's Report Card: Trends in Academic Progress 2012" (NCES 2013 456). 2013. Retrieved from nces.ed.gov/nationsreportcard/subject/publications/main 2012/pdf/2013456.pdf

National Education Association. "Research Spotlight on Peer Tutoring." n.d. Retrieved from www.nea.org/tools/35542.htm

Newcombe, T. "What Went Wrong with L.A. Unified's iPad Program?" *Government Technology*, May 14, 2015. Retrieved from www.govtech .com/education/What-Went-Wrong-with-LA-Unifieds-iPad -Program.html

Okojie, M., A. A. Olinzock, and T. C. Okojie-Boulder. "The Pedagogy of Technology Integration." *Journal of Technology Studies*, vol. 32, no. 2, 2006, pp. 66–71. doi.org/10.21061/jots.v32i2.a.1

Paas, F., A. Renkl, and J. Sweller. "Cognitive load theory and instructional design: Recent developments." *Educational Psychologist*, vol. 38, no. 1, 2003, pp. 1–4. Retrieved from cis.msjc.edu/evoc/637/References/ Pass-CognitiveLoadTheoryAndID.pdf

Rasmussen, L. "3 Ways Concept Maps Help You Learn." October 16, 2015. Retrieved from thinkeracademy.com/3-ways-concept-maps -help-you-learn/

Redford, J., K. W. Thiede, J. Wiley, and T. Griffin. "Concept Mapping Improves Metacomprehension Accuracy among 7th Graders." *Learning and Instruction*, vol. 22, no. 4, 2012, pp. 262–270. doi:10.1016/j .learninstruc.2011.10.007

Rosenshine, Barak, and C. E. Meister. "Reciprocal Teaching: A Review of 19 Experimental Studies." Technical Report No. 574. 1993. Retrieved from www.ideals.illinois.edu/bitstream/handle/2142 /17744/ctrstreadtechrepv01993i00574_opt.pdf

Schaffhauser, D. "Report: 6 of 10 Millennials Have 'Low' Technology Skills." *THE Journal*, June 11, 2015. Retrieved from thejournal.com /articles/2015/06/11/report-6-of-10-millennials-have-low -technology-skills.aspx?m=1

Schneider, J. "America's Not-So-Broken Education System." *The Atlantic*, June 22, 2016. Retrieved from www.theatlantic.com/education/ archive/2016/06/everything-in-american-education-is-broken /488189/

Sparks, S. D. "Students Must Learn More Words, Say Studies." *Education Week*, February 5, 2013. Retrieved from www.edweek.org/ew /articles/2013/02/06/20vocabulary_ep.h32.html

Stanford Teaching Commons. "Characteristics of Effective Teachers," n.d. Retrieved from teachingcommons.stanford.edu/resources /teaching/planning-your-approach/characteristics-effective -teachers

Statistic Brain. "Attention Span Statistics." *Statistic Brain*, 2016. Retrieved from www.statisticbrain.com/attention-span-statistics/

U.S. Department of Education. "Organizing Instruction and Study to Improve Student Learning: A Practice Guide," 2007. Retrieved from ies.ed.gov/ncee/wwc/Docs/PracticeGuide/20072004.pdf

U.S. Department of Education. "U.S. High School Graduation Rate Hits New Record High," 2015. Retrieved from www.ed.gov/news/ press-releases/us-high-school-graduation-rate-hits-new-record -high-0

U.S. Department of Education. "Use of Technology in Teaching and Learning," n.d. Retrieved from www.ed.gov/oii-news/use -technology-teaching-and-learning

Vanderbilt University Center for Teaching. "Teaching Problem Solving," n.d. Retrieved from cft.vanderbilt.edu/guides-sub-pages/problem -solving/

Vogler, K. E. "Asking Good Questions." *Educational Leadership*, vol. 65, 2008, p. 9. Retrieved from www.ascd.org/publications/educational- leadership/summer08/vol65/num09/Asking-Good-Questions. aspx

Worked Example Principle [Website]. 2009. Retrieved from www.learnlab .org/research/wiki/index.php/Worked_example_principle

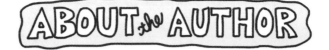

ABOUT the AUTHOR

Weston Kieschnick is a senior fellow and thought leader in Digital Leadership and Learning at the International Center for Leadership in Education (ICLE), a division of Houghton Mifflin Harcourt. Prior to his role at ICLE, he was a dean of education, assistant principal, department chair, and award-winning high school social studies teacher.

As an ICLE Senior Fellow, Weston guides districts through transforming learning cultures, empowering teachers, and cultivating innovative blended learning methodologies so that students can achieve at the highest levels while obtaining 21st century competencies and skills. School districts where he provides leadership have been recognized among the top 10 in the nation for their work in blended learning.

Weston's thought leadership around blended pedagogies has been published in *Education Week, Ed-Tech Magazine*, and *The Learning Transformation: A Guide to Blended Learning for Administrators*. He also created and hosts *Teaching Keating*, one of the fastest growing podcasts in education, where pop-culture and pedagogy collide.

Weston resides in Colorado with his wife, Molly, and his children, Everett and Charlotte.

Connect with Weston via Twitter: @Wes_Kieschnick

"Weston teaches valuable strategies for immediate implementation and provides present-day resources that boost the motivation and learning of our students. Whether his audience is four or 400, Weston engages with practicality, enthusiasm, and real-life experiences. As a teacher of nearly 20 years, I am inspired by what I have learned through his training and have found new and innovative ways to bring that inspiration to the forefront of my students' learning."
— T. Lucero, 2015 Fresno County Teacher of the Year